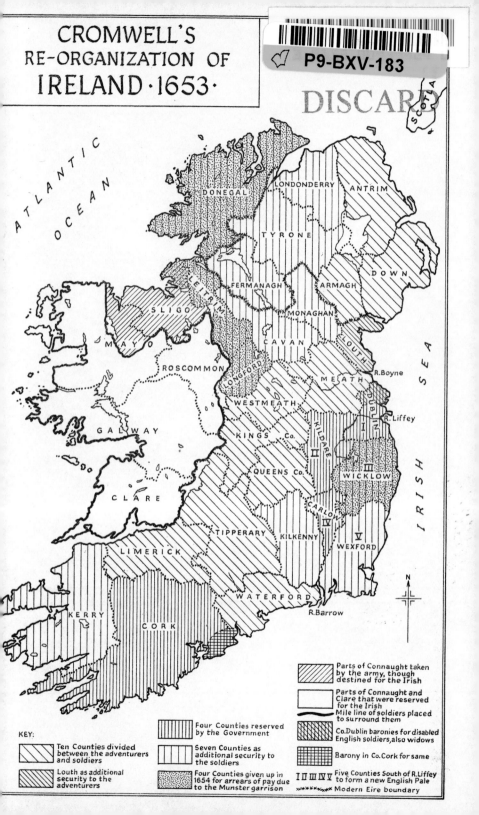

CROMWELL'S RE-ORGANIZATION OF IRELAND ·1653·

ATLANTIC OCEAN

SCOTIA

DONEGAL
LONDONDERRY
ANTRIM
TYRONE
DOWN
LEITRIM
FERMANAGH
ARMAGH
SLIGO
MONAGHAN
MAYO
CAVAN
LOUTH
ROSCOMMON
LONGFORD
MEATH
R.Boyne
WESTMEATH
DUBLIN
R.Liffey
GALWAY
KINGS Co.
KILDARE
II
QUEENS Co.
III
WICKLOW
CLARE
CARLOW
IV
TIPPERARY
KILKENNY
V
WEXFORD
LIMERICK
WATERFORD
R.Barrow
KERRY
CORK

IRISH SEA

N

KEY:

Ten Counties divided between the adventurers and soldiers

Louth as additional security to the adventurers

Four Counties reserved by the Government

Seven Counties as additional security to the soldiers

Four Counties given up in 1654 for arrears of pay due to the Munster garrison

Parts of Connaught taken by the army, though destined for the Irish

Parts of Connaught and Clare that were reserved for the Irish

Mile line of soldiers placed to surround them

Co.Dublin baronies for disabled English soldiers, also widows

Barony in Co.Cork for same

I II III IV V Five Counties South of R.Liffey to form a new English Pale

×××××× Modern Eire boundary

The Curse of Cromwell

A HISTORY OF THE IRONSIDE CONQUEST OF IRELAND, 1649-53

The Curse of Cromwell

**A HISTORY OF THE IRONSIDE CONQUEST
OF IRELAND, 1649-53**

by
D. M. R. ESSON

ROWMAN AND LITTLEFIELD · TOTOWA, N.J.

First published in the United States 1971
by Rowman and Littlefield, Totowa, N.J.

ISBN 0-87471-073-1

First published in Great Britain 1971
by LEO COOPER LTD
196 Shaftesbury Avenue, London, W.C.2

Printed in Great Britain
by Ebenezer Baylis and Son Limited
The Trinity Press, Worcester, and London

CONTENTS

MAPS

Drawn by Boris Weltman

ILLUSTRATIONS

For
CJE & LME
NJRE
TRE
and
RMRE

It is impossible to narrate the story of Oliver Cromwell and his Ironsides in Ireland without explaining the traditional policies of England, and the alternate zeal and indolence with which they were executed. In this particular context we need only go back to the day when Thomas, Viscount Wentworth, the Lord Deputy of Ireland was recalled by King Charles to bolster up his tottering regime. Wentworth's success in Dublin Castle had been marked by six years of tranquillity. Within two years, however, Hell was let loose, and misery was to be the lot of the Emerald Isle for another eight. But to the crescendo of Cromwell's guns the blight of discord was to be swept away, and the firm hand of his Ironsides laid upon her governance. In the fullness of time the Stuart family was to be restored to the thrones of its ancestors; but the consequential removal of strength and purpose from Irish government was to bring in its wake a recrudescence of misery.

The facts of Cromwell's campaign speak for themselves: but whatever judgement may be passed on the means employed to achieve victory, one great consequence cannot be ignored; the rapid restoration of order, coupled with full integration with the rest of Britain, brought in its wake one of the most prosperous periods in all the history of Ireland.

The wisdom of Cromwell's policies on the morrow of victory cannot be better exemplified than by the immediate outcry of English agriculture at the competition of Irish farmers. The passage of three centuries has altered the appearance, but not the effect of Cromwell's victories. Ireland is still dependent on British sea and air power for protection, on sterling for her economy, on the cities of the larger island for her markets, and on the whole English-speaking world for the absorption of her surplus people.

Irreconcilability remains. Although the cause has been removed, the immutability of the consequences are unchanged. Cromwell offered "Hell or Connaught"; but de Valera could only provide internment on the Curragh.

CHAPTER 1
The State of Ireland at the Recall of Strafford

THE land of Ireland is separated by fifty miles of salt water from the Welsh coast in the south, and by less than twenty from Scotland in the north. Surrounded by a sea warmed by the Gulf Stream, and regularly watered by the westerly winds, nature has given the country a fair and smiling face. The land itself has often been compared to a saucer: the rim represents the mountains which tower over most of her coastline, and the centre an enormous bog. The hills are breached, however, at intervals to drain the centre. Physically the most important breach is that in the south-west, where the Shannon runs into the Atlantic; but historically that breach in the middle of the east coast holds the clues to the dominance of Ireland. Rising on the north-western slopes of the Wicklow Mountains, the river Liffey flows in a great half-circle to discharge into the Irish Sea through this gap. At the mouth of the river stands the city of Dublin.

To the south rise the Wicklow Mountains. Except for streams at small fishing villages, the next breach in the mountain chain is in the extreme south-east, where the harbours of Wexford and Rosslare form the mouth of the river Slaney, and the harbour of Waterford those of the rivers Suir, Barrow and Nore. Thence the coastline runs south-westwards for two hundred miles to Cape Clear: it is deeply indented giving good and safe harbours, such as Youghal, Cork and Kinsale, into which flow important rivers whose valleys provide an easy access to the interior.

A wild, storm-lashed coast, deeply fissured and protected by out-lying rocks and shoals delimits the western shores of Ireland.

Through this runs the great estuary of the Shannon, that great drain which rises on the borders of Ulster and collects the surplus waters of a dozen counties before it mingles them with the Atlantic. Protecting this estuary stands the ancient fortress of Limerick. Only two other ports, the old garrison towns of Sligo and Galway, need mention on this coast.

The inhospitable coasts of Ulster cover the mountains of Donegal, Sperrin, Antrim and Mourne. The deep sea loughs of Swilly, and Foyle on the north, and of Belfast, Strangford and Carlingford on the east cover the gaps in the mountains, draining the land and providing it with maritime access. South from Ulster to Dublin the coast is sandy; in fine weather these beaches are suitable for disembarkation. This was the seaboard of the Pale, that land of English colonization which depended for its survival upon sea power. Through this gap in Ireland's natural mountain barrier there surged back and forth the tides of English invasion.

Although part of that same ethnic entity which produced the Scots, the Irish differ from their northern neighbours in a most marked fashion. With the Scots, religion was a personal matter between the Deity and the individual, made more solemn by its performance in public: with the Irish it was rather a fetish to divert punishment from sinners, those incantations of the witch-doctor which would drive away evil. Christianity brought them a uniformity of spiritual conduct, but after a thousand years its manifestations diverged again at the Reformation. By the time of Cromwell religion had an important significance: it was the out-ward and visible sign of the inward, political thought of the person. The Catholic hated the English; and the Protestant was no true native Irishman! Nor was this an over-simplification of the case. The Commonwealth was determined to obliterate Popery, to subdue and crush the Irish, to build in Ireland a Puritan society, pledged to the eradication of drunkenness and unclean living; they would put an end to Irish pretensions and eliminate, for all time, those disorders which disgraced the land.

There were three great basic sins amongst the people of the Emerald Isle—stealing, drink and women. The Irishman con-sidered that the tillage of the soil was the task of the serf: he was prepared to go without the benefits conferred by such an occupa-tion and to live from the proceeds of living creatures on meat, milk, eggs and cheese; he kept livestock and spurned the back-breaking toil which would give him bread, kale and root crops. It is true that he would grow barley, but this was only to provide him with strong liquor in which he could drown those sorrows which his indolence had brought upon his head. He spurned to dig peat when he could the more easily cut down standing timber. His fecklessness alone bade fair to devastate the land.

Amongst such people the introduction of an industrious colony, whose members would do all those things an Irishman would not, acted as an irritant. Envy at the superior station in life achieved by such colonists due to their toil and thrift soon led to stealing; stealing led to reprisals, and reprisals to that chain of hostility which is with us to this day. The natural and normal increase in population caused the Irish masses to sink further into the slough of penury and misery, from which they were only rescued by those colonists whom they so greatly detested.

With the arrival of Richard de Clare, Earl of Pembroke, otherwise known as Strongbow, in the Liffey in 1169 the attempt of the English to colonize Ireland may be said to begin. The method of colonization was to establish a Norman–Saxon–Welsh community on the eastern seaboard in order to control the foreign trade of the country and thus dictate its entire policy. The sea-port colonies were established, but there was little trade and much fighting. The native Irish strongly objected to the English policy, and they attacked any colonists who left their settlements. The only area of any economic viability was around Dublin, in the area known as the Pale: here a permanent settlement was established, but even this was foundering on the hard rock of feudal stupidity.

The fundamental basis of feudal society was a villein or serf class. This, the English intended, was to be provided by the Irish. The only way to ensure the subservience of the serfs was to remove from them any hope of improving their lot, to destroy the prospect of something better or even different. But just beyond the confines of the English colonies, in the centre of Ireland, were bogs, lakes and forests; this was a fearsome place where a luxuriant foliage concealed a frightful tangle of briars, creepers, roots and vegetation of every sort, much of it in decay. This land teemed with the lawless, where no man was the master of another, where no one considered anything other than the needs of the instant: it was the happy hunting ground of the "wild Irish". Thither fled the criminal, the oppressed, the adventurer: the latter hoped to tame a sufficient number of these marauders, to organize their depredations, and to enjoy the proceeds of their plunder. But the Irish were untameable, and the adventurer soon became as barbarous as those amongst whom he had come: it was he who became "more Irish than the Irish".

The area of the Pale expanded or contracted with the zeal of the English viceroy, the financial and military resources at his disposal, the support available from the colonists and England, the cohesion of the Irish, the strength of the antagonistic policies and the skill of those charged with their execution. Gradually, however, over the years the Pale grew to the extent of including all the land within some forty miles of Dublin. Beyond the Pale the English viceroy's authority stretched as far as his arm. Using bribes, flattery and cajolery as well as force, his influence was extended steadily westwards. But in the wake of this expansion came speculators. Like the earlier adventurers their purpose was financial aggrandisement, but their methods were very different. As soon as land was available, they settled there to organize its maximum exploitation, arranging to extract from it all it could produce. Once this was done, they imported stewards from England to run the estate whilst they moved on to repeat the process or to return to England to enjoy the fruits of their exertions. The landlord now became an absentee, and was only interested in the regular payment of his rents. But the speculators scandalously underpaid their stewards, and connived at their consequent behaviour. The stewards battened themselves on the countryside, eager only to amass sufficient funds to support their position or to go home to England. The resistance of the Irish to this behaviour led to outrages, forays and even the rare rebellion.

The dynastic troubles of the later Plantagenets reduced to a dangerously low figure the strength available to sustain the authority of the English viceroy in Dublin Castle. The Irish were not slow to seize the opportunity and the estates of central Ireland, cultivated by English direction and improved by English precept, reverted to the descendants of the dispossessed who returned from the bogs and mountains of the west. Sword in hand they were sworn to regain their ancestral possessions or to die in the attempt. The resident landlords of the area were faced with the alternatives of "going Irish" or departing. They "went Irish". These Irishized families provided the land with the most dangerous element known to the English cause, leadership. Once compromised, their interests became Irish, although their skills and thought processes remained English. What their forefathers had won by the sword, they would keep by policy; but this policy would now be Irish.

The two most important families in Ireland were the Butlers and the Geraldines, between whom the supreme power in Ireland swayed for hundreds of years; indeed, Cromwell's principal enemy was a Butler. The Geraldines controlled two great areas: the earls of Desmond occupied the counties of Limerick, Cork and Kerry; the earls of Kildare held the debatable frontiers of the Pale and most of County Wicklow. Between them lay the Butler lands in the counties of Kilkenny, Carlow and Tipperary; here the suzerainty of the earls of Ormonde and Ossory was acknowledged. Each in his own earldom lived the life of a petty princeling, owning no superior, quarrelling with his equals, and either oppressing his inferiors or disbursing largesse to them in a most open-handed fashion.

The lack of interest taken by Henry VII was rivalled only by that of his son, until the latter was stung to intense irritation by the sudden appearance of a hostile and triumphant Irish army laying siege to Dublin Castle itself. Hastily he provided an expedition to re-conquer Ireland: this force commenced the process by hanging a crowd of rebels at Maynooth in 1535. This "Pardon of Maynooth" had its effect and the rebellion collapsed. But within a year the Reformation began in England.

To wean the Irish nobility from the Church Henry VIII had to despoil the monastic houses for the almost sole advantage of this turbulent crew. Although there was no resistance, or even a sign of it, there was flung into the Irish arena a gage: it was thrown by the Pope, and the English could never really get to grips with this foe. The homeless monks went forth into the land to preach God's word, the word of the Pope, the word of Ireland, the word withal of Irish resistance. At first Dublin Castle took no notice of this, but the Fifth Column of the Papacy gained, and has since kept, the upper hand in the struggle for the minds of the Irish masses. The eradication of English heresy was the ecclesiastical counterpart to the political ejection of the English soldiery. The single influence capable of reforming the Irish character and moulding her sons into a form acceptable to civilization was affronted; the Catholic Church, denied all assistance and frequently persecuted, became the spiritual solace of the disfranchised.

The only religious counterweight to Papal propaganda was Puritanism, and its introduction coincided with a fresh source of immigration. The wild and deserted north-east coast had never attracted the English: it was of little use to them, and the Irish spurned its barren soil, but to the Ayrshire and Galloway Scot it was the Promised Land. No one would disturb their prayer meetings; there they would be free to indulge the fanaticisms of their Calvinistic faith. There began an invasion, peaceful at first, whose consequences were to disturb the tenor of Irish ways even to the present day. These Scots observed the mistakes of the English; the dispersion of their colonies, their dependence on the subject Irish, the absentee landlords and their dishonest stewards, the speculators, the inadequacies of the conflicting policies, the lack of local cohesion and all the other deficiencies. To avoid these mistakes they resolved to take only enough land for themselves, to oust the Irish, to import their own kith and kin from Scotland to take their place, and to stay upon the land they cultivated. From the first these colonies prospered; the policies upon which they were founded were sound, and succeeding generations did not change them. While the English colonies were dispersed and absorbed by the Irish, the Scots in Ulster pressed steadily on to build their concept of an ideal society. Religious troubles in Scotland kept up the supply of fresh blood from the Reformation till long after the Glorious Revolution. This colony, so different from the Pale, had a purpose so similar to that of the Tudors that Queen Elizabeth encouraged its early growth; it was a source of pride to King James; Strafford valued its steady support; the Kilkenny Confederacy did not care to disturb such a hornet's nest; Ormonde sought their aid; even Cromwell was glad to give them honourable terms. They represented, as they still do, the one enduring reality in the shifting sands of the turbulent Irish scene.

After the Reformation the alternate parsimony and vigorous repressions of Elizabeth gave Ireland a miserable period. Around her tiny garrisons and colonies surged a tide of hatred, malice and envy. The Irish hoped to swamp these outposts and sever the connection with England. But the adventurous spirit of the times prompted some West Country gentlemen to establish a fresh colony in Ireland, a fresh incursion to tame those restless Irish. They would enter the country through the southern ports, away from any restraint from Dublin; they would depend for sustenance on their own private supply lines from Devon, brought over in their own ships; they would settle in Munster and eradicate the nuisance of the Irish by simply exterminating them. The disorders which this policy provoked only made matters worse. The new colonists harried the south and slaughtered great numbers of the Irish, but they failed to eliminate all resistance. They settled on the land, but by employing the Irish to work it they sowed the seeds of their own undoing. An embittered working class, different in manners, language and religion from their masters, returned in penury to the scenes of their former prosperity to find it occupied by strangers, whose strength dwindled as their numbers were reduced by wastage and outrage. At the time of the Spanish Armada the English were, however, markedly in the ascendant; their tiny garrisons sufficiently over-awed the country to ensure that the shipwrecked Spaniards were not befriended. By one of those deplorable manifestations of national ingratitude the Irish slew most of the Spanish survivors for the sake of the gold coins in their pockets.

The first two Stuart kings took less and less interest in the country. But the turmoil grew and grew, until some action had to be taken. In the summer of 1633 a remarkable man, Thomas Wentworth, arrived in Dublin as King Charles' Lord Deputy. His administration represents six years of firm, patient, capable and courageous government. His efforts deserve substantial notice.

Wentworth, a wealthy Yorkshire landowner, had gifts of leadership and business acumen outstanding even when such ability proliferated. These talents attracted the notice of the King.

2

After serving in Parliament as a member for Yorkshire, he became one of the leaders of the popular party, and then attempted to reconcile the interests of the Commons and the Court. His reward was promotion and he became the Lord President of the North. Here, armed with ample Conciliar jurisdiction, he curbed "the overmighty subject", protected the poor, improved trade, and found work for the unemployed; in short, he repeated in York the entire vigour of the Star Chamber. His success with the turbulent north was the prelude to his appointment as Lord Deputy of Ireland, a post he filled with increasing success as one year followed another.

When Wentworth arrived in Dublin, corruption and anarchy were the rulers of Ireland. Lawlessness was common. Externally the land was defenceless, and a band of Turkish pirates had landed at Baltimore to carry off over a hundred people into slavery. The English settlers in the countryside had battened upon the land like locusts, evicting the poor and harrying the rest with higher rents. In the ports the English merchants combined to cheat the customs and to monopolize the markets, extracting the last farthing from the Irish artisan. To maintain this ascendancy the law was corrupted by bribery and the army was permitted to indulge in violent extortion. Furthermore there was no money in the Treasury.

Theoretically the Government of Ireland was a replica of the Westminster administration with a legislature of King, Lords and Commons, a Royal Executive, a set of courts administering Law and Equity, and a full ecclesiastical hierarchy. A Privy Council advised the Viceroy; it also provided him with a Star Chamber, known in Dublin as the Court of Castle Chamber. Each province of Ireland was under the executive control of a President, a rapacious brute whose independence increased with his distance from Dublin. The provincial President was responsible for the administration of the Royal estates; his example as the steward of an absentee landlord often consisted of squeezing the last mire out of the tenant, while by defalcations in his accounts he defrauded the King. Complaint was useless: the judges looked to bribes to supplement their incomes. To approach the Lord Deputy needed money, and failure was a passport to a living hell. By a wise provision of Sir Edward Poyning, Henry

VII's Lord Deputy in 1495, the Irish Parliament had been subordinated to that of England. This celebrated enactment was designed to prevent the utter ruin of Ireland and to control the rapacity of the landowners who dominated the assembly. Although Poyning's Law was to become a real and serious grievance in later years, at the time it represented a real safeguard against the wilder forms of political extravagance.

The clergy of Ireland were a very mixed lot. The Catholic priests were nominally proscribed, but their hold upon the broad masses, particularly beyond the confines of the Pale, had raised them to a spiritual edifice which enabled them to find an ample sustenance on which to live. Many landlords were Catholic; more were not unfriendly to one whose hostility could be dangerous but who would not willingly make an enemy. Materially the wandering life of a celibate, accepted as an honoured guest in every Catholic home, was a marked improvement on the barren poverty of the cabin; mentally, the respect of the peasantry was at once the reason and the reward of a calling, always hard and often dangerous. At the other end of the scale the militancy and non-conformity of the Presbyterian ministers of the north was a grave affront to the established Church, but these ministers were protected by the pugnacity of their flocks. The menace of a political alliance between them and the Catholics, both disfranchized by the penal religious laws, was a threat no government could afford to ignore. Superimposed on this was the only legally acknowledged ecclesiastical entity, the Church of Ireland. This was staffed by placemen, time-servers, adventurers, failures and such-like from England: few were really interested in their flocks spiritually; more were concerned with the tithes they could extract from the sullen peasantry, who were thus compelled to support an alien and heretical church. Many a parson went to Ireland full of zeal for the reclamation of the souls of the ignorant, but the amused indifference of the gentry and the blank refusal of the peasantry to listen drove them back, despairing, to reap the reward of a comfortable stipend and a decent house. Against the direct assaults of the Roman church they could fall back on the penal laws; against mere tolerance, indifference and contempt they were powerless.

The relationship of church and state in Europe at this time entitled the monarch to lay down the form of worship his subjects should observe. Ireland was no exception to this theory, and her laws enforced the monarch's wishes. The stern and savage legislation of England directed against the remnants of Catholicism was repeated in Ireland, where it was regarded as yet another imposition of the alien yoke. No Catholic could fill any public office, perform any public duty except to pay his taxes. He was subject to a fine if he neglected to attend his parish church on Sunday. But these restrictions would have brought the economic life of the country to a standstill, and successive viceroys had tacitly ignored their existence, except by accepting bribes not to enforce recusancy fines. But even this softening of the rigour of the penal laws was valued for what it was, an admission of failure: the English could not run the country without the help, sparse and grudgingly given, of the Irish, and by the penal laws they were depriving themselves of even this assistance.

This was the Augean stable Wentworth had to cleanse. He began by meeting his Privy Council, a truculent crowd: all were of considerable skill and ability, but they were all jealous of each other and all were hopelessly compromised with authority in some way or other. The Earl of Cork, the Lord Treasurer of Ireland, feared nothing; he organized violence and terrorized his opponents. Lord Loftus, the Lord Chancellor, was crafty, cunning and mean; his rapacity was underhand and vicious. Lord Wilmot, the President of Connaught, was a superannuated princeling grown lazy with the wealth he had acquired by force and fraud. But worst of all was Lord Mountnorris, the Vice-Treasurer; he was indolent, insolent, drunken and indiscreet; he gambled excessively, frequently cheating to guarantee his winnings. To counterbalance this gang, Wentworth introduced his friends: George Radcliffe, his secretary, was sworn in as was Christopher Wandesford, the Master of the Rolls, and Philip Mainwaring, the new Secretary of State. Wentworth was determined that the nobility should not tamper with his administration, and he had also taken steps to prevent them tampering with his reputation in England. The King had promised Wentworth that he would grant no lands, make no appointments in Church or State, and hear no appeals in law or equity without Wentworth's advice. With this, Wentworth felt well supported by friends and policy and saw no cause to worry about what went on behind his back.

The overwhelming necessity of the time was to get some money into the empty Treasury. For some time the Privy Council had been agreed that the easiest way was to soak the Catholics by enforcing the recusancy laws. Wentworth saw the political danger; it might provoke a rebellion, and would certainly antagonize the only feasible counterweight to the turbulent nobility. Accordingly he made discreet inquiries as to whether the lesser gentry would accept a demand for a benevolence, the Stuart euphemism for a forced loan, in return for a promise of fair and regular taxation for the future. Lord Balfour, an Irish Privy Council member, learnt of this and decided to oppose the scheme: a benevolence would require him to pay now, and regular taxation to pay regularly in future, which was not to his liking. He organized a petition against benevolences. Wentworth promptly accused Balfour of disloyal behaviour, deprived him of his place on the Council and ordered him to explain himself to the Privy Council in London. Wentworth was pleased with his initial success: he was now certain of replenishing his Treasury and he had shown Ireland the consequences of opposition to his wishes.

Ireland was under the hand of a determined man: who would feel the weight of his fist next? The Vice-Treasurer had not long to wait. Wentworth, his brother and Radcliffe spent the next six weeks auditing the Irish Treasury accounts. Payment of sums due from the Treasury had been made by promises to pay, backed by the anticipated receipts from taxes. These promissory notes passed as currency, and in any normal society where mutual confidence existed no difficulty would have arisen; but in Ireland there was neither confidence nor security. When these notes were presented they could not be paid, and the disappointed holder sought only to discount his bill for what he could get. Wentworth put a time limit of six months on all bills, making those time-expired void, and refusing payment before the named date. Confidence returned, and a further breathing space was obtained for the disordered Irish economy.

The Lord Deputy now turned his attention to the army. The troops were ill-fed, rarely paid, and almost never clothed; under these conditions desertion was common. The deplorable messing led the troops to supplement their rations by poaching, and then by cattle rustling, and then to every other sort of depredation. The officers, often in the same plight as their men, were no better and frequently worse. Training and exercising were non-existent. Wentworth first saw to it that this rabble was paid; he then ordered them to exercise. There was no small alarm among the officers about this, for many had never seen their troops. The inspections of the Lord Deputy would disclose their gross inefficiency, and the examination of their muster rolls would expose their direct corruption. Wentworth directed that all troops would do duty in Dublin for varying periods throughout the next two years; he would thus see for himself how his reforms were working. The natural martial qualities of the Irishmen, coupled with correct treatment by their officers, transformed this mob of banditti into a brigade of real soldiers, the hard core of Royal power in Ireland. The two thousand infantry and the thousand cavalry were improved in quality and increased in strength as year succeeded year until a division of some eight thousand disciplined troops stood ready to do the bidding of the Lord Deputy. The improved behaviour, the steady bearing of the soldiers soon became a matter of remark to the Irish; and the army ceased to be the last resort of the desperado and the social outcast.

The Lord Chief Justice, Lord Kilmallock, had brought his career of oppression and rapacity to a culmination by convicting an obviously innocent man of murder in order to obtain his lands. Wentworth dismissed him immediately. He also attended to the administration of the law. As with the army he ensured that the judges were promptly paid, and so by increasing their salaries he put them beyond the reach of bribery: but he also insisted that they should attend to their business and ensure that those who sought justice should get it.

The Court of Castle Chamber had been created by the Tudors for the same basic purpose as the Star Chamber, to curb the over-mighty subject. Queen Elizabeth had invested it with power "to receive, hear and determine all bills, complaints, supplications and informations ... concerning riots, routs, forcible entries, unlawful assemblies, deceits, perjuries, forgeries, defaults, falsities, misdemeanours of sheriffs and other officers, contempts, disorders, misdemeanours and offences committed . . . in Ireland", with authority to punish offenders with "fines, imprisonment or otherwise", to compel witnesses to appear and all the other adjuncts of legal authority. This could solve Wentworth's problem: no longer would the turbulent nobility bribe judges, suborn juries, intimidate witnesses, browbeat sheriffs, disperse litigants as if they were rioters or indulge in any other of the time-honoured practices of the Irish legal system. Wentworth persuaded King Charles to extend the jurisdiction so that Wentworth sitting alone might hear purely civil cases. So to the Court of Castle Chamber came the litigants of Ireland; here there were no court fees, no bribes, no intimidation; ruthless and relentless as the decrees of this court were, they were essentially just, and the people of Ireland knew it. Here the truculence of the baronage and the merchant oligarchs was severely punished: all the exactions and oppressions, all the arrogance and repressions evaporated before the power of Wentworth's Castle Chamber, the supreme engine of the new autocracy.

Like all competent rulers Wentworth had an efficient intelligence service which provided him with timely information on all the plots, subterfuges, cabals, intrigues and tricks which subsisted in the morass of Irish life. Like all such services it was secret, and across the gap of three centuries we have little knowledge of its organization. But the very success with which Wentworth's policies were crowned showed that he knew the reaction, in advance, of every person of note in the Irish hierarchy, both lay and clerical, to any suggestion he might make. His agents told him that about two out of every three Irishmen were active Catholics; that amongst the English, the lesser gentry and the smaller merchants were tired of the excesses of the great men; and that the broad masses of the Irish would welcome any form of government provided it was both firm and consistent. Here were the corner-stones on which the Lord Deputy could form a policy to keep the King's Peace in Ireland.

Tolls on highways and at bridges, cesses at markets, harbour dues and similar charges were arbitrarily fixed by their owners and altered with every passing whim. Wentworth stopped all this. By order of the Privy Council owners were forbidden to charge more than a reasonable fee for the facilities offered. It was well understood that disobedience would lead to a summons to appear in the Castle Chamber.

Under the impact of these reforms the economic life of Ireland began to revive: the country people found that they could take their produce to market without having to pay an exorbitant cess; they could work their farms to capacity without having their rents raised; the lesser gentry found that the suppression of disorder enabled them to enjoy a modicum of comfort; the smaller merchants enjoyed the improvement in trade; now that the blights of faction were removed all could plan ahead and look forward to even more profitable times. Within twelve months of his arrival Wentworth felt he could turn his attention to the legislature. In return for the initial benevolence he had promised to reform the fiscal system and put it on to a generally acceptable basis; the time had come to redeem this promise.

Wentworth required the permission of the King before he could call a Parliament, and as this was during the King's Personal Rule in England, the prospect of an Irish Parliament sitting in Dublin was unlikely to appeal either to the King or to the English Privy Council. Accordingly the Lord Deputy carefully briefed his young brother before sending him to London to obtain the necessary authority. After the whole situation had been explained to him and the risks evaluated, King Charles gave his permission. The news when it broke took Ireland by surprise. It was Wentworth's intention to have a Parliament nicely balanced between Catholic and Protestant, between Celt and Saxon, between the middle classes and the peasantry. With a small nucleus of Crown nominees he could dominate the assembly, and crown his decrees with the appearance of their being the will of the people democratically expressed in the proper way. The elections were rowdy and corrupt; but Wentworth had arranged that the interests of the Crown were not ignored. The results came fully up to his expectations: and what was more, no one could say he had packed his Parliament; but he had balanced it.

On 14 July 1634, Wentworth opened Parliament with all the trappings of ceremony and splendour. In the Speech from the Throne he outlined his programme of reform, gently insinuating that it was really the King's. He asked for money, pointing out that all these plans required expenditure, and since it was for their benefit and not the King's, it was not unreasonable for them to bear the cost. He indicated that if they wished to go even further their zeal for the welfare of Ireland would receive support from above. An inquiry into the iniquities of the land question might follow when time for the investigation of these scandals could be found. In effect, in return for supplies, this new Parliament could have a free hand with legislation; this was the theory, but Wentworth had solid grounds for believing that he could manage legislation through his own nominees and a prudent distribution of patronage. He ended by urging his hearers to support the Government. "Divide not between Protestant and Papist; divide not nationally, betwixt English and Irish. The King makes no distinction between you, reputes you all without prejudice and that upon safe and true grounds . . . his good and faithful subjects . . . Above all divide not between the interests of the King and his people. You might as well tell me an head might live without a body . . . as it is possible for a King to be rich and happy without his people being so likewise. Their well-being is individually one and the same, their interests woven up together with so tender and close threads, as cannot be pulled asunder without a rent in the Commonwealth. Remember therefore I tell you, you may easily make or mar this Parliament."

Except for the turbulent nobility, all Ireland was delighted and Parliament gladly voted the necessary subsidies. Wentworth went further: it was arranged that taxes should be assessed and collected throughout Ireland under the direction and control of the House of Commons. This ensured that the great landowners and the merchant princes would disgorge their ill-gotten wealth, and would not be allowed to off-load the burden on to the shoulders of the down-trodden peasantry and the artisans. The Lord Deputy thereupon promised Parliament that this Irish money, raised by Irish taxation, should not be used outside Ireland. It was to require all Wentworth's skill with the King and all his ability with the English Privy Council to keep this promise, for the English Treasury was almost perpetually empty.

In plenty of time for the harvest, Wentworth prorogued Parliament, fixing the next meeting for December: the financial business had been settled and it only remained to complete the

legislative programme for the Lord Deputy's reforms to be complete. During the viceroyalty of Lord Falkland, his predecessor,
King Charles had in effect sold a charter of some forty clauses to
the settlers for £20,000. This charter, known as the "Graces",
gave them an immunity to harry the Irish in any and every
possible way. Three of the clauses referred to the antiquated
system of land tenure, and entitled the baronage to evict those who
held their land on dubious titles. For the previous five years the
baronage had enforced these provisions in a most cavalier
fashion, or merely used them as a cloak to conceal their depredations. Wentworth knew that he had to get these "Graces"
cancelled before he could attack the land scandals. The Privy
Council was browbeaten into the acceptance of this policy; but
when Parliament reassembled one Privy Councillor, Sir Piers
Crosby, revealed that he had not been convinced by the Lord
Deputy. In the Commons he inveighed against the new policy.
The King had granted these boons, who did Wentworth think he
was to cancel them? On this narrow constitutional question Sir
Piers swung the Commons behind him, and progress on all other
reforms was stopped. Wentworth was thus compelled to offer
the Commons a Commission on Defective Titles in return for
the cancellation of the "Graces". The trick worked, but this was
the Commons treating with the Lord Deputy on equal terms, and
not Wentworth rewarding them for obeying his orders. Sir Piers
was dragged before the Castle Chamber, deprived of his position
as a Privy Councillor and imprisoned for his temerity: but
Wentworth had not heard the last of his truculence. The reform
programme included a legislative ratification of the Privy Council
orders on the various tolls, cesses and dues, a complete re-
organization of the system of land tenure and conveyancing, a
prison building scheme and arrangements for prisoners to be
employed on public works and an investigation into the State
pension system as well as the Commission on Defective Titles.
By Easter 1635 the work was complete and Parliament was
dissolved.

Wentworth had wooed and won the Irish: he had also made a
number of influential enemies, who would one day hound him
to the scaffold. Although the older families of the Anglo–Irish
peerage had approved of Wentworth's policies, they made it

abundantly clear that the methods he used could not be repeated
on them, and they would tolerate none of his arrogance. Their
leader was the young James Butler, Earl of Ormonde. After
Wentworth had referred in derogatory and disparaging terms to
the "conquered Irish", Ormonde approached him privately to
warn him not to repeat the insult. To prevent unseemly brawls
Wentworth had ordered both the Lords and Commons to leave
their swords at home when they attended Parliament. Ormonde,
relying on his privilege as a peer, refused to obey: he told the
doorkeeper at the House of Lords who asked for his sword that
he could have it "in his guts". Summoned to appear before the
Court of Castle Chamber for this disorderly and disobedient
conduct, Ormonde refused to apologize and justified his actions
by producing the patent of his peerage which entitled him to
appear armed in the presence of the King. Here was an enemy
Wentworth could not kill. Adopting the principles of Machiavelli,
Wentworth made a friend of him, had him sworn of the Privy
Council and admitted to the secrets of the Court party in the
House of Lords.

In the midsummer of 1635 Wentworth himself, virtually an
itinerant Castle Chamber, began a progress through the country
to investigate the titles on which land was held. He began in
Connaught. In the morass of juristic casuistry involved it was
impossible to do complete justice, but Wentworth did what he
could. Whenever he was in doubt he would confirm an honest
tenant's title. But for the unscrupulous adventurer who had
grabbed what land he could on some nefarious pretext, or none at
all, the Lord Deputy had no mercy. The land was declared to
have reverted to the King. He had little trouble until he reached
Galway. Here he found Lord Clanricarde tampering with a jury
to obtain a favourable verdict. Infuriated with this behaviour
Wentworth arrested the sheriff, fined the jurors, foisted a military
garrison on the town, and had the case retried, when the verdict
was favourable only to the Crown. Clanricarde fled and died
shortly afterwards; the bulk of his lands were escheated to the
Crown. For the resettlement of the hundred and twenty thousand
acres thus acquired Wentworth was determined to find small Irish
farmers in spite of the multitude of pressures put upon him by the
English Privy Council and even the King himself. It was his

intention that these small men should form a yeoman class, at once self-supporting, independent and free from dependence on the great magnates. To discourage speculators and absentees he required guarantees of both cultivation and residence from all grantees.

The restless Deputy now turned his attention to the mal-practices of the merchant oligarchs who controlled the municipal corporations of the seaport towns and enforced various trading monopolies. The leading burghers in these towns had formed self-perpetuating governments, controlled by themselves, but funded from oppressive rates and other exactions from the lesser merchants and the artisans. They allowed harbours to silt up, the streets to go uncleansed, the public edifices to deteriorate. They took no interest in local life except for what they could squeeze out of it, and if commodities grew scarce, they would not hesitate to corner all the supplies in order to make the greatest possible profit. Wentworth forbade this behaviour and when he was disobeyed the heavy and relentless arm of the Court of Castle Chamber was stretched forth to punish such temerity.

The liberalization of trade necessitated the suppression of the monopolies. Many of these monopolies belonged to absentees whom Wentworth could not reach; they could, and did, react violently to his intended interference with their property. He found that the easiest way to break a monopoly was to support breaches of it. He proclaimed that the wool-staplers had no sole right of purchase. He refused to permit the export of corn and butter in famine years. He prevented the formation of syndicates to exploit monopolies in tallow and tobacco. The fall in prices and the rise in the standards of living of the Irish was the direct result of this policy, and it raised the prestige of the Lord Deputy to new heights among the Irish. But, of course, in doing so he had made more enemies, and these among the influential courtiers in England.

Finally Wentworth set about investigating the affairs of the Church of Ireland. The Thirty-Nine Articles were imposed, an Irish Court of High Commission set up, and the parasites who had infiltrated into rich livings were ejected. The administration of the Irish Church had been a quagmire, but gradually order and decency were restored; the lazy and the pluralists were put to work, the scoundrels were unfrocked, and provision was made for the spiritual life of the nation.

But the most remarkable thing about the administration of Wentworth was his religious tolerance. In an age when legislation about thought was rigidly enforced with all the means at the disposal of the State, he resolutely refused to permit the enforcement of the anti-Catholic laws. The Irish knew the result: no petty tyrannies would disturb their worship, no stupid recusancy fines would hit their pockets, no more would ecclesiastical informers make life a misery for Catholics. In return Ireland enjoyed tranquillity.

Among the enemies Wentworth made were the two great men of his original Privy Council, those he had resolved not merely to discredit but also to humiliate. The first of these was Viscount Mountnorris, the Vice-Treasurer. Wentworth had begun by scrutinizing his accounts so closely as to indicate that dishonesty was suspected. As one of the great magnates of the country, various sinecures were within the gift of Mountnorris, and a commission in the army had accordingly been granted to his nephew. Young Annesley was the usual type of high-spirited subaltern and his conduct on one occasion was felt to be worthy of rebuke by the Commander-in-Chief himself. All would have been well if the Commander-in-Chief had not also been the Lord Deputy. Since Wentworth had not been trained as a soldier his rebuke was resented and young Annesley received a second rebuke for dumb insolence. Another Annesley was a page in the household of the Lord Deputy. This youth was singularly clumsy and he managed to stumble on Wentworth's foot when it was inflamed by gout. The incensed Viceroy, not unnaturally, cursed the boy roundly. Under normal circumstances no one would have connected the two incidents, but Lord Mountnorris felt that the Lord Deputy was minded to insult the whole Annesley family. Shortly afterwards Mountnorris got drunk when dining with Lord Loftus and while in this condition he roundly abused the Lord Deputy. Amongst the sinecures Mountnorris himself held was the colonelcy of a regiment and thus was subject to military discipline. Wentworth learnt of this outburst at the time but did nothing about it for eight months. Then when it might be anticipated that all had been forgotten, Wentworth had Mountnorris suddenly court-martialled for uttering public threats amounting to treason. Within the hour the Vice-Treasurer was under sentence of death. Although Wentworth had no intention of having Mountnorris shot, equally he had no intention of letting him go until he had apologized unconditionally. Try as he would, and he tried very hard, Mountnorris could not persuade the Lord Deputy to relax the stranglehold and in the end he did apologize. More was to be heard of this incident later.

The second case was one of the gravest scandals imaginable, nothing less than the deliberate and dishonest interference of the Lord Chancellor himself with the course of justice. As the other great men were being humbled and compelled to surrender their ill-gotten gains, the greedy Lord Loftus felt that this was merely opening up the entire field for himself and he was not going to allow such uncontrolled scope for rapacity to slip through his fingers. Acting through nominees Lord Loftus arranged for some Crown lands in Wicklow to be granted to the O'Tooles and the O'Byrnes in return for suitable consideration. This was discovered by Wentworth, and although the matter was concealed from the public, the grant was annulled. A little later a certain John Fitzgerald was involved in a land suit which should have been tried in the Court of King's Bench but Lord Loftus decided to try the cause himself in the Court of Chancery, and in camera. Here poor Fitzgerald was bullied unmercifully, being most wrongly deprived of his rights to call witnesses and be heard in his own cause. When he protested at this treatment he was imprisoned for some five months for contempt of court. When he was finally released from prison, Fitzgerald complained to the Lord Deputy. This was just the sort of strong meat that Wentworth enjoyed chewing. Lord Loftus was summoned to appear before the Court of Castle Chamber. Not being accustomed to having his actions questioned by the Lord Deputy or anyone else he refused to appear; nor was Wentworth accustomed to having anyone, even the Lord Chancellor himself, treat the Court of Castle Chamber with contumely. Sustained by the Privy Council Wentworth dismissed Lord Loftus from office and demanded the surrender of the Great Seal. Loftus hid the Great Seal and prepared to leave Ireland secretly; Wentworth's intelligence service warned him of this and Loftus was arrested.

Concurrently with this incident another unpleasant interlude was being played out. Wentworth was enjoying a fairly harmless flirtation with the Lord Chancellor's daughter-in-law, whose sister was married to George Wentworth. The idle dalliance within the family circle might never have come to the notice of the world, but in spite of the shame he brought on his own family Lord Loftus was not to be slow in compromising the Lord Deputy. It so happened that the girl's step-brother and guardian visited Ireland, where he discovered that the rents guaranteed by Lord Loftus under the marriage settlement of his son and daughter-in-law had never been paid to the young couple. Loftus refused to discuss the matter with the guardian who was also a trustee of the settlement. Accordingly the latter commenced an action against the Lord Chancellor. When Lord Loftus announced that he would try the case himself, and in camera, Wentworth intervened to transfer the case to the Court of Castle Chamber. Loftus began by being truculent and ended by losing. Therefore he appealed to the English Privy Council.

Wentworth had always regarded it as a cardinal principle of his policy that he need never fear the consequences of an appeal from his justice. But now if Wentworth allowed Loftus to go to London over the marriage settlement affair, he also allowed him to escape from the consequences of the Fitzgerald case. So he refused Loftus permission to go to London until he had surrendered the Great Seal and purged his contempt. Loftus complained to his friends on the English Privy Council, and Wentworth was ordered to facilitate his journey. Ignoring this Wentworth wrote to the King explaining that he must enforce obedience before he could allow Loftus to leave. Once the matter was made clear to him the King supported his Lord Deputy. Unsustained, Loftus now abjectly submitted, surrendered the Great Seal and resigned his office. He went to England and put about the story that he was the victim of an intrigue of the Lord Deputy and his mistress. This malevolent gossip was to sustain the prejudice which would cost Wentworth his life and Ireland years of misery.

In the year before Wentworth became Lord Deputy the Irish customs yielded £22,553 to the Treasury: in the first full year of his administration it leapt by nearly 70% to £38,174, and three years later it reached a peak of £57,387. The enormous debt owed by the Irish to England was reduced steadily during his administration. In 1634 he remitted £4,692 to London; four years later the annual sum had risen to £10,441. For Charles I this was a more than welcome addition to his threadbare Treasury.

For the re-granting of sequestered lands Wentworth did not get from the King the support which he should have had. The courtiers who had lent the King money to sustain his policies wanted their money back; the dispossessed sought to re-acquire their lands; the adventurers wanted profitable investments for their surplus funds; all nurtured hopes of reaping some of the rewards of the increasing prosperity of Ireland. The King found it increasingly difficult to resist these pressures, particularly when they were urged upon him by the Queen, or his favourite clerics like Archbishop Laud. The young Earl of Clanricarde, the son of the rogue Wentworth had caught suborning a jury in Galway, successfully obtained a re-grant of his family lands. Protest as he might Wentworth was forced to acquiesce.

During the Personal Rule of King Charles, England was quiet until money ran short. Some of the King's expenditure was on a new navy, and to build it he re-imposed the ancient tax known as Ship-Money, the feudal obligation of the seaports and the maritime counties to provide for external defence. Because he felt it was an unfair burden on the coastwise community, King Charles decided to levy the tax on the entire country. There was uproar. Some of the gentry refused to pay, and as a test case the King ordered his Attorney-General to prosecute John Hampden, a popular and agreeable Buckinghamshire landowner. The case came before all the Judges of England in the Court of Exchequer Chamber, where five of the twelve sustained Hampden's refusal to pay. The King's victory was Pyrrhic, Hampden became the hero of the hour, and financial resistance was the new policy of the broad masses of Englishmen.

One might be forgiven for thinking that a Scottish King would take a more than passing interest in the welfare of his compatriots. Machiavelli would have revelled in a situation where a single monarch united in his own person two hostile nations, separated in creed, law, thought, history, manners and economy. But King Charles was to throw away this priceless boon and attempt to reduce Scotland to a mere shire. Driven on by the pig-headed Archbishop Laud, Charles tried to unify Britain by interfering in the affairs of the Scottish Kirk: they were to use Cranmer's prayer book and accept the direction of the bishops thrust upon them by King James VI. But the Presbyterian ministers had too tight a hold on the affections of the masses for the scheme of a Sassenach. The Scottish people were determined not to bend the knee to this, the first instalment of Popery. Was not the King's wife a Catholic? With great skill and ably assisted by the Kirk the anti-court party obtained the overwhelming adhesion of the Scottish people. The Scottish creditors of both Stuart Kings had followed their monarchs to London where they had persistently reminded them of their obligations. They had retained a close connection with their native land, and they now found themselves asked for advice by their English counterparts. They correctly gauged the temper of the English nation, and reported their findings to Scotland. Primed with this information, armed with a good cause, sustained by the enthusiasm of the people and supported by ample funds, the Scottish leaders resolved that they would not submit; they were satisfied that the King could not make them do so. In the early spring of 1638 the old Confession of Faith was redrawn into the form of a national political manifesto, and signed with every possible form of solemnity. It was the written determination of the nation to reject all alien impositions, especially in religion. Yet still King Charles fondly imagined he could bend the Scots to his will. A riot had occurred in St Giles Cathedral in Edinburgh the previous year; now the nobility were openly siding with the people. The King sent the Marquis of Hamilton north to convoke a General Assembly of the Kirk to settle matters, while he himself began to raise an English Army to coerce the Scots. But by the end of the year the General Assembly was out of hand, and the King had no English Army!

The Scottish Covenanters, named from the "Solemn League and Covenant" they had signed the previous spring, had summoned home the battle-hardened mercenaries from Germany where they had been fighting under Gustavus Adolphus in the Thirty Years War. The Scots soon had as fine a little army as was to be found in the British Isles: their only counterpart was the

3

army of Ireland, but this was smaller and had not the same cohesion. In the Scottish Army, officers and men alike were Covenanters; in the Irish, the officers were still mainly Anglo-Norman Protestants, the men Irish Catholics. By May 1639 the Scottish Army, fully equipped and trained, was concentrated just north of the river Tweed, ready to invade England.

Opposed to the Scots south of the Tweed lay the English Army. King Charles had ordered the Lord Lieutenant of every county to send the appropriate contingent of troops to join the Royal Army on the march for the north. The orders were obeyed grudgingly or not at all. The country gentlemen who might be expected to officer the force refused to turn out, or if they did, with such a lack of enthusiasm as to be a drag upon its efficiency. The rank and file were in a worse state: they were neither paid nor fed. To remedy this, they stole. Such behaviour further depressed the regard for Royal authority, and the difficulties of raising and maintaining the army continually increased. The hectorings, cajolery, pleadings, persuasions of the Royal officers, whether for recruits, money or supplies were met with refusals: some were rude, others were obstructive, many were sullen, and most were contemptuous. In spite of this widespread defiance, King Charles persisted, and his untrained polyglot rabble was directed to the Scottish border. Here they were to be exposed in the presence of a larger, better-trained and disciplined army to the effects of a well-directed propaganda. This came from two sources: the Scots indicated clearly that battle meant destruction; their empty stomachs indicated that to stay where they were meant starvation. Those who had been induced by specious promises to enlist were not to be deterred by ferocious decrees, as worthless as the paper on which they were written, from desertion.

The lesson of the times was not lost upon Ireland or any of the different peoples who lived there. It had long been felt by the Irish that "England's danger was Ireland's opportunity". Every faction in Irish life knew that every other faction would be preparing for a struggle, narrow and partial in its objects; no faction would be prepared to sink its differences. Before Wentworth's eyes stretched a vista of waste, desolation and misery. The chaos with its black-mail, murders, rapine and all the other adjuncts of weak and hesitant rule loomed up to set at naught the patient work and hazardous toil of six years of capable and fair administration. The old rascals were not averse to a return to the days before Wentworth when they and no one else had the field to themselves. The Scots in Ulster were keen to support their compatriots. The English settlers were not immune to influences hostile to the concept of Personal Rule. But the Irish knew only too well that the Lord Deputy alone stood between them and the most arrogant exploitation imaginable, economically synonymous with slavery and socially with imprisonment.

As Wentworth digested the news that came with every ship across the Irish Sea, he became more and more aware of how badly the King had handled every opportunity of sustaining his policy of Personal Rule. The ungrateful Scots should never have been provoked into defying him in religious matters; the stubborn English would now only goad him into impotent fury; only the Irish remained loyal. In Wentworth's hands lay a key to the solution, the crowbar with which the King, captive in his own land, might prize open the Anglo-Scottish clamp, the Irish Army. It could hardly coerce Scotland, but it could defend England, and it might prevent the disloyalty of the countryside from becoming a menace to the Government. If King Charles agreed, Wentworth, still the Lord President of the North, could teach the Yorkshire gentry a sharp and salutary lesson. He wrote to the King and urged his policies. Keep the English quiet at all costs, and then use the Irish Army to blockade the Scots. But events were moving too fast. The substance of Wentworth's despatches became known in Scotland due to the irresponsibility of the Marquis of Hamilton. The English Army was useless and its commander incompetent; the people were on the verge of rebellion, and the Treasury was empty. Without having to fight a battle the Scottish Army was triumphant. The King could only make peace.

Couched in terms of subservience, flattering to the King but deceiving no one, the Pacification of Berwick was agreed in June 1639. The Scots agreed to disband their army, to restore their fortresses to the King, and to dismantle offensive fortifications. The King agreed to call off his naval blockade, to liberate his prisoners, and to restore all confiscations. A General

Assembly and a Parliament was also convoked for the ensuing August.

Meantime Wentworth had been having some troubles of his own. The Earl of Antrim, of Scottish ancestry and sympathy, obtained from the King a general authorization to recruit an army in Ireland. He demanded assistance from the Lord Deputy, and suggested that he might second regular regiments. He explained that his purpose was to invade Galloway, an area already under the military control of the Marquis of Argyll, and he insinuated that this was a duty imposed by all Kings upon their Deputies in Ireland in the terms of their commissions. But Antrim's real purpose was to sustain his kith and kin in southern Scotland against the King's pretensions: and well Wentworth knew it. It would be enough to sustain the loyalty and zeal of any Irish mercenary to know that he fought against the English, particularly if he was regularly paid; within the coffers of the Covenanters there was plenty to do this. All these considerations were clear to Wentworth, and by his own diplomatic skill he managed to redirect the energies of Lord Antrim elsewhere. He suppressed in the nick of time an insurrection in Donegal; and he managed to extinguish some incipient disaffection among the Scots of Ulster.

In the summer of 1639 Wentworth set out on a viceregal progress of northern Leinster. Aiming to visit all towns within thirty miles of Dublin, his itinerary was arranged so that he could keep in close touch with external affairs and not be taken by surprise if his presence was needed in Dublin. He reached Naas, a straggling market town about twenty miles from Dublin where the roads to Limerick and Cork diverge, on 5 August 1639. That evening a messenger brought him a despatch: "Come when you will, you will be welcome to your assured friend, Charles R." This was a Royal Command, and Wentworth hastened to obey.

Wandesford and Robert, Lord Dillon, the heir of the Earl of Roscommon, were sworn in as Lord Justices, the ancient officers who fulfilled the functions in the absence of a single holder of the viceroyalty. The Earl of Ormonde was given a Marquisate and the command of the army with young George Wentworth as his Chief of Staff. After making these arrangements Wentworth left Dublin for London on 12 September 1639. The mailed fist wrapped in a velvet glove had been removed from the helm of Ireland. Ten years were to pass before Ireland would feel the weight of another mailed fist. In the meantime many things were to happen.

For the history of Ireland prior to the Stuarts, I have relied on:
Rev. E. A. D'Alton: *The History of Ireland*, 6 Vols. (Gresham, 1910).
Sir Shane Leslie: *The Irish Tangle* (McDonald, 1946).
The Irish Administration of Wentworth is described in detail in his biographies, and in many of the standard works covering the affairs of Ireland at this period. Particular mention should be made of:
Lady Burghclere: *Strafford* (London, 1931).
Dame Veronica Wedgwood: *Wentworth* (London, 1935).
Dame Veronica Wedgwood: *The King's Peace* (London, 1955).
S. R. Gardiner: *History of England, 1603–1642* (London, 1883–4).
Earl of Clarendon: *The Great Rebellion* (Oxford, 1885).
The Clarendon State Papers, Vol. 1 (Oxford, 1872).
E. Kearney: *Strafford in Ireland* (Manchester, 1959).
J. O'Grady: *Strafford in Ireland* (Dublin, 1923).
R. Bagwell: *Ireland under the Stuarts* (London, 1916).
The patent creating the Court of Castle Chamber can be found in:
G. W. Prothero: *Statutes and Constitutional Documents, 1558–1625* (Oxford, 1894), pp. 150–153.
The "Graces" can be read in:
A. Clarke: *The Old English in Ireland, 1625–1642* (London, 1966), Appendix II, pp. 238–254.
The Scottish National Covenant is to be found in:
S. R. Gardiner: *Constitutional Documents of the Puritan Revolution, 1625–1660* (Oxford, 1889), pp. 124–134.

CHAPTER 2
The Massacres of the Protestants

Wentworth had been recalled, not in disgrace, but in triumph. His policies in Ireland had been successful: his policies for England were the only alternative to an abject surrender by the King. If he were successful in England, the Irish magnates knew he would be back to humiliate them again. At all costs Wentworth, they said, must be destroyed: there was no weapon they would not use, no stone they would leave unturned. There would be no restraint; no quarter would be given.

Wentworth found the plight of King Charles deplorable. There was either sullen resignation or triumphant contempt everywhere. Taxes could only be collected by the courts and bailiffs; there was no social disgrace in defrauding the revenue. Towering above all else the barely tolerated Scot was no longer considered a locust who had followed his King to London to fatten himself on the lush pastures of the south, he was a fellow creditor of an untrustworthy bankrupt. Both the Scot and the Englishman were in the same sorry plight. They were affronted in religious matters, they were denied a hearing in temporal concerns, they were hit hard in the pocket, and they had no redress. King Charles had consummated the policies of the Plantagenets and the Tudors for the union of the two peoples, with the important exception of imposing his own supremacy. The most influential of both nations had a common purpose, limiting the Royal powers. It was Wentworth's task to re-establish the Royal authority, and to provide the means of executing the Royal policies.

After Wentworth's arrival in London the first occurrence of

note was the appeal of Lord Loftus, which was unanimously dismissed; but Loftus remained in England where, joined by Lords Cork and Mountnorris, he spread rumours derogatory to Wentworth. Most were those dangerous three-quarter truths which are so difficult to refute since they are so largely based on accepted fact. A superficial observer might think Loftus was wasting his time, but he was not; he knew his future in Ireland would be decided in England; he was going to make sure when the time came that the decision was favourable to himself.

The Pacification of Berwick was only an armistice, and now commissioners from both sides met to discuss the peace. Both the King and Wentworth felt that the Scots wanted too much, and when Wentworth was appointed to the English delegation, it was easy to make the negotiations end in deadlock. Sir John Coke, the Secretary of State, was made the scapegoat for the failure and he was dismissed. He was replaced by Sir Harry Vane, then a secret member of the anti-court party and no friend of Wentworth. It was the policy of both Wentworth and Vane that the treaty negotiations should fail. Wentworth wanted the Scots to renew the war with a major invasion of England and thus provoke the English into support of the King. Vane hoped that the new war would lead to the calling of a new Parliament.

For his great services the King now created Wentworth Earl of Strafford and Lord Lieutenant of Ireland. The latter was a new office and its duties included the discharge of all Royal functions in Ireland as well as those traditionally performed by the Lord Deputy. These marks of Royal approbation were to give Strafford further confidence as he set his face towards the future, the dangers of which it is as well he could not clearly see.

The two pressing needs of the King were men and money; the two sources were England and Ireland, and the two means were the calling of their Parliaments. Strafford knew he could obtain anything from the Irish Parliament; with such an example he hoped to be able to do the same in England. His advice was accepted. In March 1640 Strafford opened a new Irish Parliament in Dublin. His opening speech from the Throne was received with the most extravagant and universal enthusiasm. Here was no suppliant Lord Deputy begging for the financial means of supporting his weak administration; the King's personal representative was having thrust upon him the wealth of Ireland and the promise of her riches as well. Nearly £200,000 was voted within three days, and with this went the good wishes of the Irish legislature. The Commons explained that their zeal was due to the good and courageous administration of Strafford in the past, but their action was probably tinged with the thought that an Irish Army would soon stand on English soil, giving the English a sharp taste of military medicine.

After a fortnight in Ireland Strafford returned to London. The Irish Parliament had been prorogued until June, by which time it was hoped that the English Parliament would have been brought round to a similar state of mind. When Strafford, who was suffering from diarrhoea which made travelling slow and uncomfortable, reached London the King had already opened Parliament. But there was no desire in England to exhibit any financial generosity. The King was now between the Scylla of bankruptcy and the Charybdis of invasion. He had reached this position by his own acts; Parliament's price to redeem him again was likely to be high. They intended to sit upon the purse strings until their grievances had been redressed; and the list of these was long. The new House of Commons was filled with such men as Hampden, Pym, Vane and a Huntingdon farmer, Oliver Cromwell. The request for money was met by a demand for a statute declaring Ship-Money illegal. Strafford advised the King to appeal to the House of Lords; the advice was accepted, and the device was successful. The two Houses were now divided, and the King ought to have been able to play the one off against the other. Strafford opposed any bargain with the Commons, suggesting that the King ask for an absolute minimum of funds after which he could withdraw Ship-Money as a favour, but it must not be a "bribe to brawling moneylenders". For immediate use £350,000 was wanted; within the foreseeable future £750,000 would be required. The Privy Council finally advised the King to ask for £500,000 in the first instance. Thereupon for some reason not now known Sir Harry Vane offered the House of Commons in the King's name to withdraw Ship-Money in return for £750,000. The policy of Strafford, the strength of the King's position collapsed in an instant; the King could only dissolve Parliament.

The Short Parliament was dissolved on the morning of 5 May
1640. That afternoon a Privy Council was summoned at Whitehall to discuss Scottish affairs. The King presided; Strafford,
Laud, Sir Harry Vane and a few others were present. As
Secretary of State, Vane took a note of the discussion. The
Pacification of Berwick had not been formally denounced, but a
fracas at Edinburgh showed clearly that the Scottish Covenanters
were preparing to re-invade England. The Privy Councillors,
mature and able men, were despondent until Strafford spoke.
Since the Scots were determined to crush the King and could not
be deterred by policy, he urged that they had no choice but to
"go vigorously on". The only chance lay in a sudden and immediate attack; he urged the use of his Irish Division. "You have
an army in Ireland you may employ here to reduce this kingdom.
Scotland shall not hold out five months. One summer well employed will do it. I would carry it or lose all." Parliament had
refused to vote any taxes, so the King must use his prerogative
and enforce Ship-Money again. He must tell the people that
Parliament was useless to protect them from the Scots, but he
would do his best. The Lord Lieutenant of each county must be
told to raise his quota of forces and to place them at the
disposal of the King. The Star Chamber was also to be instructed
to quash any incipient insubordination. The very vigour of the
policy and the determination of the man heartened the King,
infused new life into the Privy Council, and indicated to the
nation that "Tom the Tyrant" was in charge and would brook no
interference with his plans.

Strafford's policy might just have succeeded if he had been left
in full control of affairs. Unfortunately his diarrhoea got worse
and he then developed pleurisy. In his absence the Privy Council
was leaderless for two months. The Scots, probably by treachery,
knew what was happening, and were taking the appropriate
remedial action. When Strafford finally returned, he found affairs
were virtually beyond control.

In England the county levies were either refusing to turn out,
or were refusing to leave their counties. The countryside was
refusing to find billets for troops, forage for their mounts, or to
make weapons; the gentry were cynical and contemptuous. In
Scotland the Covenanters' Army, supported by the enthusiasm of

the whole nation was moving steadily southwards into England. They were furious at the faithlessness of the King, and they were barely resisted by the conscripted ragamuffins who formed England's Army. In Ireland the position had deteriorated. Ormonde had taken leave to look after his sick wife, and his position was filled by George Wentworth, but George had to leave Dublin regularly for troop inspections, exercises and so forth, and this loosened Strafford's hold on Irish affairs. All was made worse when the King gave way to the importunings of Lord Cork by making him an English Privy Councillor, and appointing Colonel Goring to the Irish Army Council. The House of Commons had begun to quarrel, and the great landlords were busy with bribes and bullyings to advance their interests.

Strafford wished now to go back to Ireland to restore order in his own way, and to return with the Irish Army at his back. But Lord Northumberland, the English Commander-in-Chief, was now taken ill. The disgraceful condition of the army required the services of an outstanding leader, and the only man fit to fill the post was the Earl of Strafford. His policy was sacrificed on the altar of expediency; through no fault of his own he was to find himself in an impossible position. At the end of August 1640 he arrived in York to assume the command of the English Army. First he had to find some money to pay the troops. He had to infuse some fighting spirit into them; he had to arrange some training: he had to restore discipline; he had to drive out the Scots, and he had to ensure the tranquillity of his own rear.

Somehow Strafford managed to extract a little money from the Yorkshire gentry, but this was his only success. He then left for the Border counties: but the Scots had forestalled him. On 28 August the Scottish Army began to cross the Tyne just west of Newcastle. English attempts to repulse them were driven off with ease, and soon the Scots were marching down the road to York. There was little fighting: the unpaid and leaderless troops fled, spreading tales of woe; the local gentry were delighted that the thieving poaching mob were going and a disciplined army, the Protestant veterans of many a German field, would soon be taking their place. So far had the wheel turned that the hated, dreaded Scots were coming as friends and liberators. Strafford had lost, and his enemies were delighted.

Twelve English peers now pressed their petition on the King to call a new Parliament. They averred that the King was spending the nation's money on a war of which they disapproved; they objected to the ecclesiastical discipline of Archbishop Laud, to the continuation of Ship-Money, to the irregular grants of monopolies, and to "the long intermission of Parliaments". They expressed the gravest concern about the plan to bring over the Irish Army. They ended with a threat: the new Parliament would investigate "the causes of these and other great grievances . . . and the authors and councillors of them may be there brought to such legal trial and condign punishment as the nature of the several offences shall require". The King could not bring himself to accept this advice; instead he called a Great Council of the Realm, a body co-extensive with the House of Lords. But this only postponed the day when Parliament had to be called. To eke out the remaining time with funds the King managed to borrow £200,000 from the City of London, but to this loan was attached the conditions of peace and a new Parliament. Strafford wanted to use these funds to launch a last desperate attack upon the Scots, but this was beyond even the faithless Charles. Writs for a new Parliament were then issued.

On 3 November 1640 King Charles opened the Long Parliament. In membership it closely resembled the previous one: in its early life Pym was its unchallenged master. In his speech from the Throne the King urged the necessity of ejecting the Scottish Army whom he described as rebels, ascribed the poor state of the English Army to lack of funds to pay the troops, admitted that grievances existed, and suggested that financial liberality would be the means of rectifying the ills of the nation. Pym and his friends, however, felt that the presence of the Scottish Army in northern England was just the balance to Royal pretensions that they needed, that the existence of a Royal Army was a threat to their liberty, and that by voting funds to restore its discipline they would augment the threat. They were anxious to keep the King so short of money that he would be helpless in their hands: the rectification of each grievance would be paid for, but at their price. Only the most adroit management could preserve the semblance of Royal prestige. Only the most accomplished politician could be at once the leader of Parliament and a personal devotee of the King. Only one man could do this, if he were allowed to try, and many were prepared to deny him this chance. At his master's bidding a sick and dejected Strafford came to London.

On the evening of 10 November Strafford arrived in London. Pym's spies quickly brought him the news. Here was the defeated and discredited Strafford delivered into his hands. He could not escape, the mob would see to that; the King could not protect him, Parliament would see to that; he could not protect himself, Pym was determined to see to that. The following morning Pym persuaded the House of Commons to sit in secret. Once the doors were locked he developed an attack on his rival; he complained of the way the country had been run over the past twelve years. "There was one more signal in that administration than the rest, being a man of great parts and contrivance . . . a man who in the memory of many present had sat in this House an earnest vindicator of the laws, a most zealous champion for the liberties of the people. He is become the greatest enemy to his country and the greatest promotor of tyranny that any age has produced: the Earl of Strafford, Lord Lieutenant of Ireland and Lord President (of the North)". He instanced the tyrannies of Strafford's behaviour in York during his administration there. He inquired why an army 8,000 strong had been raised in Ireland and suggested that some of his repressions had been for the purpose of gratification of his mistress. Most of his hearers were stern, unbending Calvinists. Strafford could no longer be "in grace", he was damned; no sympathy with his misfortunes could be shown; it would be doing the Lord's work to drive him to destruction. Sir John Clotworthy, an Irish rascal who represented Maldon, supported the attack. He complained of Strafford's arrogance in Ireland, and all the incidents of his autocracy were recounted anew in their most unfavourable light. Why had Sir Piers Crosby been imprisoned? Why had recusancy fines not been exacted? What about the way Lords Clanricarde, Loftus and Mountnorris had been treated? News of what was afoot leaked out, but when Strafford learnt of it while closeted with the King, he said, "I will look my accusers in the face". He left to take his seat in the House of Lords but was intercepted on the way by Black Rod and impeached by the Commons of England of High Treason.

With Strafford safely confined in the Tower of London, Pym could embark on his programme of preventing the King from ruling without the consent of Parliament. Those who had assisted in the exercise of arbitrary power were to be punished; all the instruments of tyranny were to be destroyed. In the process the absolute authority of Parliament would be asserted, and a weapon more terrible than the dreaded Star Chamber was to be used. After removing the Chief Minister, Pym attacked the lesser lights. Archbishop Laud was sent to the Tower. Lord Chancellor Finch was impeached, but he managed to escape. Francis Windebanke, the Queen's secretary, did not wait to learn his fate, but crossed the Channel in a rowing boat during a thick fog. All monopoly owners were expelled from the House of Commons. Opposition to King Pym in the future was likely to be as severely treated as opposition to King Charles in the past.

By now the affairs of Ireland were drifting. Wandesford was a very sick man and quite unable to control the old magnates. In the middle of November he heard of the impeachment of his friend. It broke his heart and on 3 December 1640 he died. The common people of Ireland wept, for the last barrier between them and the abyss had gone. The Irish House of Commons was soon out of hand; urged on by Strafford's enemies they prepared a petition, known as the Irish Remonstrance, complaining of the exactions and the autocracy of the past eight years. The Remonstrance was brought to the English House of Commons: whilst between the Puritans of England and the Irish riffraff there was a wide moral gulf, their immediate policies were the same, and this was grist to Pym's mill. The menace of Ireland, prosperous, powerful and devoted to the King, could easily be removed by giving the old factionaries a free hand to create trouble; if there were quarrelling, the prosperity and power of Ireland would soon be dissipated. The economic threat to England's agriculture and industry was as powerful an anti-Irish influence as the fear of an Irish incursion; Pym would eliminate both. It was also necessary to silence Strafford's friends in Ireland: Gerald Lowther, the Lord Chief Justice of Ireland, Richard Bolton, the new Lord Chancellor, George Radcliffe, Bishop Bramhall and Thomas Little, Strafford's Irish secretary, were all impeached; they were thus debarred from giving evidence at Strafford's trial.

The Earl of Cork had by now made an Irish magnates party in the English House of Commons. This coterie ensured that the petition of any and every discontented man in Ireland should be noticed in the Parliament of England: they were not slow to grasp the opportunity. The judgements against Lords Loftus and Mountnorris were reversed, and these two blackguards were free to re-inflict their presence upon Ireland. These men had schemed and plotted their revenge for years and now they gloated over their opportunity.

The English House of Commons devoted most of its time during the winter of 1640–41 to preparing the indictment against Strafford. The preliminary stages were completed in time for the trial to begin on Monday, 22 March 1641 in Westminster Hall. In the meantime, Pym had been perfecting his plans to transfer the Royal authority to Parliament. The first great measure he pressed through Parliament was a Triennial Act: this ensured that there should be "no intermission of Parliaments" for more than three years and if the King omitted to call one for any reason, the Lord Chancellor or the Lord Keeper would be in duty bound to issue the necessary writs for doing so. Pym now felt reasonably secure since the King was not going to dissolve Parliament once he had got some money and thus spoil his chances of getting the rest. Such a policy might save Strafford and slaughter Pym. The formal trial on impeachment dragged on into April with various delays caused both by Pym's determination to obtain a conviction and Strafford's intermittent sickness. By 10 April 1641 the difficulty of proving the case was all too apparent and to the Puritan Commons the prospect of an acquittal was all too painful. On many of the charges Strafford had proved his innocence; on others he had thoroughly discredited the evidence for the prosecution. Their first attack was in danger of failure; Strafford would go free and would assuredly take a terrible revenge. When the trial was adjourned on this day, the Commons returned to St Stephen's Chapel where Pym now opened a second line of attack—a bill of attainder.

Pym explained that Henry Vane, the son of the Secretary of State and one of the burgesses for Hull, had found the minutes of the Privy Council meeting of 5 May 1640 amongst his father's papers. Pym read the note. Without a doubt Strafford had intended to use the Irish Army to coerce England and here was the proof. What "here" and "this kingdom" meant mattered little; in the last resort Strafford could be handed over to the Scots if these words were intended to apply to Scotland only. If they applied to England, and of that the Commons would be the judge, then Strafford's words deserved death. Henry Vane then explained how he had stumbled across this document, how he had long considered what he should do with such dread knowledge and how he had finally concluded that it was his bounden duty to bring it to the attention of the House of Commons. Sir Harry Vane was furious and rounded on his son for such unfilial behaviour, but the House was not interested in family disputes. This interlude served, however, to keep the father in his appointment as Secretary of State until December when King Charles saw his duplicity at last and dismissed him. The way was now clear. The party of Pym could not permit Strafford to live; he had to be destroyed and the means were of no importance. Sir Arthur Haslerig now formally introduced the bill of attainder which he had already prepared and it was read a first time. In mounting excitement the English and Irish nations watched as the impeachment continued whilst the attainder bill was being pressed through the House of Commons. Using all the arts of a demagogue and all the skills of a party politician, Pym pressed the third reading through the House on 21 April. On 26 April the House of Lords gave the bill a first reading and the next day it was read a second time. Over Easter the Houses were adjourned. The mob in Westminster and London, thirsting for Strafford's blood, reached unmanageable proportions. To strengthen the hands of his supporters Pym now pressed a resolution through both Houses of Parliament requiring their members to take an oath "to maintain and defend . . . the true reformed Protestant religion . . . against all Popery . . . to maintain and defend His Majesty's royal person and estate, as also the power and privilege of Parliaments, the lawful rights and liberties of the subjects . . . and to endeavour to bring to condign punishment all such as shall by force, practice, councils, plots, conspiracies or otherwise do anything to the contrary . . . and in all just and honourable ways endeavour to preserve the union and peace betwixt the three kingdoms of England, Scotland and Ireland." Those who failed to take this oath were excluded, and resistance to the policies of Pym was at an end. On 8 May the House of Lords gave the bill a third reading by 37 votes to 11.

King Charles had promised, not once but many times, that Strafford should have both his life and his honour. On 23 April he had repeated this promise in a secret letter, but the contents were betrayed and the mob clamoured loudly for the fallen minister's blood.

On 4 May Strafford realized his end was near: the country was convulsed and the King would be helpless if he refused to assent to the attainder. Pym would probably order the Serjeant-at-Arms to execute the sentence of both Houses. With the King thus defied in his own capital, all England would be adrift. He would go with dignity and perhaps King Charles would benefit. He wrote to the King: "I understand the minds of men are more and more incensed against me ... To set your Majesty's conscience at liberty, I ... beseech your Majesty, for prevention of evils which may happen by your refusal, to pass this bill." On 10 May, after struggling to avoid the dreadful responsibility, King Charles signed the bill. At the same time he approved a bill preventing the Dissolution of Parliament without its own consent. Two days later Thomas Wentworth was beheaded on Tower Hill. Pym had effectively removed an engine of English despotism, and all Ireland was adrift.

After the death of Wandesford, King Charles had appointed Lord Dillon to take his place, but Dillon's brother had married Strafford's sister, so Parliament compelled the King to revoke the appointment. The Government of Ireland then fell into the hands of the Lord Justices; they were Sir William Parsons, Master of the Court of Wards, and Sir John Borlase, Master of the Ordnance. They were well-meaning men, but far too weak to control the mighty forces which were soon to rend Ireland. Later the King appointed the Earl of Leicester to the vacant position of Lord Lieutenant.

The King still had the Irish Army and Pym knew that he had little time to lose if he were to blunt that weapon. He represented to the King that it was undesirable to maintain such a vast force

Thomas Strafford, 1st Earl of Wentworth

King Charles I

to keep in order such a tranquil Ireland; since it was composed of Catholics it could have no interest in maintaining a Protestant connection; and unless military and financial economies were effected in Ireland the English Commons would find it difficult to vote any further funds. The King was thus compelled to order the demobilization of his Irish division. An establishment of 3,000 men, similar to that maintained by Wentworth's predecessors, was approved for Ireland; the keen, native and competent soldiers of Wentworth were disarmed, disbanded and dispersed. Their arms and those for replacements and reserves, enough in fact for at least a division, were stored in the vaults and cellars of Dublin Castle. Some of the men thus discharged went abroad, but most stayed in Ireland to provide a nucleus for the hard core of Catholic dissidents.

In the debatable borderlands of central and southern Ulster where Scottish and English colonists had pushed steadily onwards dispossessing the Irish as they went, a long series of proscriptions, settlements, outlawries and resettlements had bred numerous deep-seated injustices. Here the ferocity of the Scot had been restrained by the civilization of the English settler, but the bitter, irreconcilable and enduring hatreds of the Irish remained. Amongst the partially dispossessed Irish was the family of O'Neill, the holders of the Earldom of Tyrone. One of the Earl's nephews was Owen Rory O'Neill, commonly called Owen Roe; he was serving in the Spanish Army in Flanders whence his fame had spread back to his native land. When he learnt of some plans to oust the English he promised to return. Another of the family was Sir Phelim O'Neill. He had been educated in England as a Protestant, but the severe discipline of the Puritans was not to his liking, so he reverted to the ancient faith on his return to Ireland. The descendant of a rebel he still smarted under the Elizabethan lash of forty years before; a member of a noble family, he was a natural leader; as a Catholic he relished the prospects of crushing Protestants; and as an Irishman he was ready for any desperate enterprise. Other firebrands in the family were Sir Henry O'Neill and Hugh and Emer MacMahon.

The re-introduction of recusancy fines in Ireland alienated the entire Catholic Church. By shelving this question, Wentworth had removed one bone of contention in Ireland. But now the Irish

4

The principal areas concerned with the uprising are those to the South and West of Lough Neagh. It was here that the most ferocious and savage actions took place.

Treasury became dependent on the financial persecution of the Catholics. Among the militant elements of the priesthood was Emer MacMahon: then the Vicar-General, he was later to become Bishop of Clogher, a diocese in central Ulster, the very heart of the disaffected region. He had been one of the sources of Wentworth's information and was well aware of the devious routes by which government information travelled in Ireland, and of the stranger methods by which it was obtained.

These O'Neills and their friends, including Lord Maguire of Enniskillen, Phil O'Reilly and Roger Moore of Leax, decided to harness this powder-keg of Ulster ill-will, which had been exacerbated by religious persecution. They prepared a plan to evict the English from all Ireland and to take over the government. They knew that King Charles wanted to re-create the Irish Army so that he would no longer be at the mercy of the English Parliament; that he had suggested to Lords Ormonde and Antrim suitable plans to seize Dublin Castle. Since these two nobles were in touch with the Catholic leaders, the conspirators had a good knowledge of what was thought in the Royal camp. They had been prudent enough to include some priests in their midst, thus harnessing the intelligence and communications system of the church, which was of virtually unassailable security. With the information available to these men in the summer of 1641 they felt they had to act, and act quickly.

The arms cache in Dublin Castle was to be seized in a surprise attack, timed to coincide with a rising of the Ulster Irish. By the combination of surprise and overwhelming force, both the northern province and the Pale would be at their mercy overnight. The adhesion of the three remaining provinces could be expected, almost without a struggle, within a few days. If serious fighting broke out, then the Irish division could be rapidly re-formed and rearmed to crush such opposition. But the greatest feature of the rising lay in its timing. The old Irish quarter day, when taxes and rents were paid, was 1 November; immediately prior to this the peasantry would be "in funds", whilst both the government and the landlords would be living on credit. It was essential, therefore, to rise before this date so that the peasant could be rewarded by not having to pay his rent; the conspirators thus appealed both to his patriotism and to his cupidity. Saturday,

23 October would be market day in Dublin, so that the presence of a number of strangers would go unnoticed in the vast throng in the city; the introduction of the rebel troops would thus be effected, and the value of surprise would be obtained. This day was fixed for the start of the rebellion. Lord Maguire, Roger Moore and Hugh MacMahon would command the Dublin party; Sir Phelim O'Neill was to capture Derry and Sir Henry Carrickfergus; Sir Con Magennis was to seize Newry, and the local peasantry were to be urged to rise and eject the settlers.

As with every cabal in Ireland, and in spite of all precautions, some knowledge of what was going on leaked out. During the summer Sir Harry Vane learnt of the King's plans to seize Dublin Castle: he warned the Lords Justice to keep alert. The Earl of Cork knew of most of the intrigues of Ireland, and he prepared against these by amassing a reserve of ready cash. Sir William Cole, a Fermanagh magistrate, was also aware of the existence of some serious conspiracy, and he exerted every effort to discover its details, warning both Dublin Castle and the local Protestants. As a result of his probes, on 21 October he learnt that there would only be one day more of peace. He sent off an urgent message to Dublin to warn the Lords Justice of the imminence of the rising. The messenger was waylaid on the road and the message was not delivered, but the attempt on the Castle had already been foiled. Sir William also summoned his Protestant neighbours to assemble in Enniskillen and their timely obedience saved both them and him; indeed Enniskillen, and not for the last time, was to be a haven of order and refuge in a sea of insurrection and chaos.

Made privy to the plot just before the rising, and carefully rehearsed in the details of the plan to carry Dublin, Owen O'Conolly was in fact a Presbyterian elder; he was in fact a Protestant zealot! He had no great love for the English, but he bore them no great hatred. An Irishman, he well understood the consequences of a Catholic and Irish administration; he knew that they would deny him any form of religious freedom, and their repression would be far worse than that of any English viceroy. He considered the matter deeply, debating within himself where his duty lay. Finally on the evening of 22 October he went to Dublin Castle. Presenting himself at the gate he requested an interview with Sir William Parsons. Some accounts say that he had to make the request twice; others say he was drunk; but late that evening he reached the presence of the Lord Justice and there he divulged the full details of the plan. This was the news that Parsons dreaded but at last he knew exactly what was in the wind and when to anticipate the blow. Summoning his colleague, Sir John Borlase, they discussed the situation. It would be stupid and suicidal to trust the troops of their depleted military establishment to give them any form of protection; the mounting arrears of their pay had destroyed their discipline and sapped their loyalty. There lay at hand, however, a far more reliable section of the population, the English merchants and settlers of the Pale. Within the hour messengers were rousing these Protestants from their beds and summoning them to arms. When the rising began the storming party would have a warm reception.

The situation of the Lords Justice was indeed parlous; they were about to be attacked in their own fortress. They had had just sufficient warning and just sufficient assistance was at hand; without a doubt they could beat off the initial attack, but beyond the city of Dublin the entire administration of Ireland was about to collapse. The fear of the Royal dominance of Ireland had led Pym to reduce the strength of the Irish Army to insignificant proportions. The example of Pym in destroying the Court of Star Chamber and the other engines of Royal tyranny in England had been followed by the abolition of the Court of Castle Chamber in Ireland. The supply of fresh blood from both England and Scotland had stopped due to the troubles in those countries and this threatened the very survival of the Ascendancy. The Irish of the south and west were restless and would break out into open insurrection if the Ulster Rising was successful. If the Irish rose, it would be impossible to hold either the surviving English or the Scots in check. Old accounts would be settled with the bullet or the dagger, and the consequential disorders and reprisals would be quite uncontrollable. In the dire emergency with which they were faced, the only policy available to the Lords Justice was to defend themselves and leave the settlers to their own devices. The reassertion of English supremacy might take a long time; it would be enough to survive until then.

As the awful night wore on, the merchants of Dublin arrived at the Castle in increasing numbers, and it soon became apparent that there was more than ample strength in the garrison to beat off any attack. Accordingly it was decided to arrest the leaders of the revolt. The three chiefs were surprised and seized, but Roger Moore escaped. He was just in time to warn the lesser lights of the rebellion in Dublin and to call off the attack. They immediately left Dublin to avoid arrest.

Not knowing that the attempt on Dublin had failed, the conspirators in Ulster began their insurrection at dawn. Gangs of armed Irishmen descended on the homes of most of the English settlers that morning. The leaders had instructed them vaguely to throw out the English who, if they resisted were to be killed. The Irish were to be encouraged to reoccupy their ancestral lands. A soundly based revolution is generally founded on a land settlement. The new proprietors of the land can thus be depended upon to defend their acquisitions with great tenacity. The leaders also realized that the action taken by the Scots would probably decide the issue as they held a balance of power, but it was here that their hesitations and their errors were to cost them dear. The original instructions were to leave the Scots alone and at first this order was generally obeyed. But the Scots were Protestants and their sympathies were strongly inclined towards the English. Here they were wise, for the Irish were urged on to their destructive work by priests denouncing heresy generally. In the first surprise the Scots were not molested and afterwards it was too late.

The evictions were foul and ferocious. A stormy autumn heralded a bitter winter and into this, stripped of all they possessed, sometimes even of the very clothes from their backs, were flung the surviving English. Those who had resisted were dead and those who were left had to take their chance as best they could. Within twenty-four hours the rebels were in general control of Ulster and were invading the northern parts of the Pale itself. Sir Phelim O'Neill had surprised and captured Charlemont, then believed to be the strongest fortress in the north. Newry, Tanderagee and Dungannon were in flames, and Drogheda was besieged. Warning had reached Belfast, Coleraine, Carrickfergus and Derry just in time, and behind their walls the Protestants sheltered in safety. Starving, they yet held the essential sallyports through which sorties to reconquer the insurgent province could be made.

The ejected colonists sought shelter from their neighbours. If these were English their plight was the same; if they were Scots they found shelter and their stories whipped up the ancient determination of the Scots to slaughter the Irish without further ado. "Had you but allowed us our heads in this matter," they said, "there would have been no Irish to create disturbances!" Yet others sought out those Irish with whom they had lived in peace and friendship for many years, but there their reception was dreadful; they were either driven away or detained to be handed over to the lawless bands who had appeared like locusts in the countryside.

As the understanding of what they had done penetrated the minds of the ignorant peasantry, so did an understanding grow of the sort of reprisals they might expect. Within a week the practice of ejection was seen to be stupid: a despoiled and embittered man could return in a very dangerous mood; supported by the law and armed with modern weapons, his enmity could be terrible. Either the colonist must "go Irish" or he must be killed. In the killing neither man, woman nor child was spared. Indeed the Irish blood-lust went on to destroy everything English; the farms were burnt, the horses ham-strung, the cattle slaughtered. The Irish were bent on obliterating everything English, or that had even a semblance of being English. Nothing was sacred, nothing was to be spared. Wooden structures were burnt, stone buildings were torn down, and it was enough that a dog had prowled round an English midden for it to be killed; sufficient that a hen had laid eggs for an English table for its neck to be wrung.

The Protestants of Enniskillen were sturdy Anglo–Scottish yeomen who regarded themselves as particularly superior men, fit to tame the Irish and determined to do so. They felt it was their duty to uphold the honour of Britain and they were not going to allow an unseemly Irish brawl to deter them. They could see the consequences of dispersion and disunion as the firmest form of discipline. Holding the defile between the two branches of Lough Erne, they felt they need never fear a simultaneous attack from both north and south and they were certain that the Irish lacked the organizational ability to co-ordinate such action. Furthermore the Irish would never know the direction of their sallies. Elated by their successful survival, goaded by the cruel excesses of the Irish, and infuriated by the murders and plunderings, the Enniskilleners began to strike back. Foraging parties left the safety of their lines to harry the Irish, driving off cattle and sheep, ravaging the kaleyards, burning the cabins, and killing any who interfered. For long they had no news of their co-religionists: a hundred and ten miles of bad roads and hostile territory separated them from Dublin, and nearly thirty from the safety of the sea at Ballyshannon. Had they known of the massacres on the borders of Fermanagh and Tyrone, where the bodies of over two hundred English, distinguished by neither age nor sex, had been flung into the river Blackwater, their raids might have been even more terrible. As it was they were limited to making the task of an investing army impossible: all the sinews of siege warfare would have to be dragged laboriously to Enniskillen, and there the besiegers would find neither food, nor forage, nor shelter, nor services. The garrison were certain the Irish had no suitable equipment, that its manufacture was beyond the ignorant kern, and that it could not be bought for lack of funds. At the very worst they could hold out until help came.

In the initial rising Charlemont Castle was carried by an Irish attack. Lord Caulfield was captured there and later killed. Searching through the booty, Sir Phelim O'Neill found a charter signed by the King and sealed with the Great Seal. The original writing was erased, and a commission was forged. With this in his hands Sir Phelim announced that what he did was in the name of the King.

News of the rising spread through the rest of Ireland like wildfire. From Ulster came tales of sudden, incredible wealth, tales which lost nothing in the telling. Within a month Counties Wicklow and Wexford were ravaged by Irish freebooters. By the end of the year all Munster was in revolt; only Kinsale, Cork and Youghal, each with an English garrison, remained loyal. But the value of surprise had been lost, and the warning had not fallen on deaf English ears. Concentrating their families and protecting them and their portable goods in great convoys, bands of English settlers uprooted themselves and made for Dublin. These convoys were too strong for the Irish to attack, but stragglers were killed, and foraging parties were resisted. As the convoys approached the capital, foraging became more difficult, while within the city itself food was scarce. Exhausted by the journey, the refugees found little in Dublin beyond security from an Irish skean in their backs: famine and disease took as terrible a toll as the fury of the Irish. Many who survived the journey collapsed starving in the streets of Dublin. The very lucky ones, with money or influence, crossed to England. Similar scenes, on a much smaller scale, were to be seen in the other ports of Leinster and Munster.

News of the risings had been sent to the King, who was in Edinburgh, and to the English Parliament. Soon all England and Scotland knew what was afoot. The Earl of Leicester, still in England instead of doing his duty in Dublin, summoned his Council when he heard the news. They formally communicated this the next day to the House of Commons who were aghast; they had troubles enough of their own without more from Ireland. At first they were uncertain of what they should do, but soon letters came from the King. When he had heard of the Ulster rising, he realized at once that this was no squalid Irish brawl, but a determined and well-planned rebellion. He knew what to do, and he had the means to do it. He ordered General Munro with a brigade of Scottish infantry, 1,500 strong, to go to Ulster and re-conquer that rebellious province. He wrote to the English Parliament and told them what he was doing. For once the King and Parliament were in agreement: the Irish must be crushed. The King's promptitude infused spirit into the House of Commons, who resolved to sustain the Lord Lieutenant with men and money. But the agreement between the King and parliament was short-lived; his intrigues in Ireland were suspect, and his Catholic wife was suspected of meddling in the affairs of Dublin. The tales of the refugees reaching London added to this belief, and the interrogations of Lord Maguire and Hugh MacMahon only added fuel to the fire. The English House of Commons soon began debating their own grievances, known to history as The Grand Remonstrance, allowing Ireland only occasional notice.

The King left Edinburgh in the middle of November, to be received with enthusiasm by the City of London ten days later. This led him to treat the Grand Remonstrance when it was presented to him with ill-concealed disdain. In the accompanying petition the Commons requested the King "to forbear to alienate any of the forfeited and escheated lands in Ireland which should accrue to the Crown by reason of this rebellion". In reply the King "much doubted whether it were seasonable to declare resolutions of that nature before the events of the war were seen: however he thanked them for their advice, and conjured them to use all possible diligence and expedition in advancing the supplies thither, the insolence and cruelty of the rebels daily increasing". But quarrels now began over the control of the army to be raised for the reconquest of Ireland. A few companies were raised and sent to reinforce the Dublin garrison, and an act impressing more troops was passed. Another act was passed to deprive the rebellious Irish of their lands and to sell these to debenture holders. These debenture holders were to advance money immediately and were to be repaid either in land or the proceeds of its sale after the suppression of the rebellion. Among the debenture holders were John Hampden and Oliver Cromwell who subscribed £1,000 and £500 respectively. This money was to be used to finance the expedition.

The surviving colonists had not been passive in their fortresses. At Carrickfergus some colonists with the aid of a few soldiers raided Island Magee in January 1642, killing thirty rebels who had omitted to guard themselves. In Dublin Sir Charles Coote raised a band of colonists to scourge the rebels of the Pale. They followed this up by a raid into the Wicklow mountains where they shot or hanged as many Irish as they could catch. They effectively depopulated the region, removing much of the direct menace to Dublin. But Coote's force was too small for him to venture very far, and without a supply train to have gone further would have courted trouble.

In Ulster General Munro's Scots began slowly but methodically to drive the Irish out of Antrim and Down. They intended to exterminate rather than punish the Irish, so their progress was very slow, and it was further delayed by their consolidation of all their conquests as they went. Munro resisted the importunities of the settlers to launch a great drive against the O'Neills. He would not be caught in the bogs of central Ulster where he might starve, and where the conquest of some peat-hag could benefit neither his troops nor his government.

By the spring of 1642 something approaching a stalemate had
been reached. The colonists still held Kinsale, Cork and Youghal
in the south, Dublin and Drogheda in the east, and half a dozen
strongpoints in Ulster. The insurgents still held the rest of the
country; but their own depredations and violence had reduced it
to a wilderness. Here troops of starving kerns fought with each
other for such scraps of food as their own improvidence had
not destroyed. The depopulation of those parts where heavy
fighting had taken place naturally reduced the capacity of the
warring factions, but not their ferocity. Whenever armed columns
entered hostile territory they indulged their destructive capacity
to the full. On balance this operated to the advantage of the
English since they could always obtain supplies from across the
sea, but the Irish were solely dependent upon the produce of their
own land. Varying estimates have been made of the slaughter,
which range from 30,000 to over 500,000. These figures are based
on a total population of a little over a million. The smaller number
represents a very conservative figure of those actually killed by the
sword in the initial uprising; the larger may only be a slightly
exaggerated total death roll from famine, pestilence and war until
the restoration of order. Anyway at least a sixth of the total
population of Ireland disappeared from the face of the Earth that
winter, and the survivors swore to continue the killing. The process of depopulation had begun, and it was to continue by these
and other methods for another ten dreadful years. Meanwhile
the fortresses could not be reduced; nor could they in their turn
eliminate the menace of the Irish.

In January 1642 some 1,500 English troops had reinforced
Dublin; they were followed in February by another 3,000. With
the former Ormonde went to Naas, laying waste the country and
carrying back to Dublin what he could. An attempt had been
made a little earlier to relieve Sir Henry Tichborne with his English
garrison in Drogheda, but the reinforcement of 600 troops had
been surprised at Julianstown and cut to pieces. In March
Ormonde tried again; he drove Sir Phelim O'Neill from his camp
and relieved the town. Sir Henry now pursued his besiegers and
managed to capture Ardee and Dundalk. Ormonde now turned to
sweep northern Leinster as far as Athy. On his return he met some
Irish insurgents at Kilrush. A furious fight followed during which

the superior discipline of the English overcame the impetuous courage of the Irish, who were driven off with over 700 dead.

In the far south Sir Warham St Ledger, the President of Munster, had been bottled up in Cork, and the Boyle family in Youghal. At the end of the year St Ledger broke out and started a really savage career of reprisal; he executed fifty men in Waterford without trial simply because they were Irish; he drove off livestock and destroyed everything else. The Irish were just as bad; they had captured Cashel, killed most of the English there and thrown out the remainder. The survivors had a terrible journey of over sixty miles through a wasted countryside to Cork.

In the early stages of the rebellion the Catholic gentry of the Pale wished to remain loyal to the English connection. The lax enforcement of the penal laws had grown into a tacit toleration of the Catholic faith; the firm administration of Wentworth had enabled them to enjoy the benefits of civilization. They were appalled by the passage across their lands of starving and shivering refugees making for Dublin, for it might be their turn next. In spite of both religious and secular inducements to "go Irish", they decided to resist the bands of Irish rebels. They asked Parsons and Borlase for arms to protect themselves, but after these had been issued, they were recalled. In the view of the English Parliament all Catholics, whether peasants or peers, were rebels at heart, and all must suffer the consequences; the Lords Justice conformed. In December Parsons had summoned these gentry to Dublin, but they refused to obey and met instead at Swords, a village some eight miles to the north. Parsons ordered them to disperse; they did, and then threw in their lot with the rebels. A preliminary meeting was held in the middle of the month with the leaders of both sides at the Hill of Crofty. A further meeting a few days later at Tara confirmed an alliance between these two dissimilar groups. Freedom of conscience, defence of the Royal prerogative, and the equality of Ireland with England formed the core of the agreement, which put the gentry in their natural place at the head of the National Forces. Lord Gormanstown became the Commander-in-Chief, and the other peers were rewarded with important commands. Unfortunately they decided to justify their actions in writing and this had a disastrous effect in England. They drew up a petition to the King, stated the hardships they had borne, the dangers they faced, assured him of their loyalty, and proclaimed their willingness to make any sacrifice; in return they asked for the redress of their grievances. Their petition was ignored.

The gentry now began to organize the peasantry, trying to mould them into a disciplined force. But the old bug-bear of the Irish, fraternal strife, made this a difficult task. In Munster Lord Mountgarret cleared the last of the English out of Kilkenny, Waterford and Tipperary, but then he quarrelled with Lord Roche over the matter of plunder. This resulted in Mountgarret refusing to fight any further and retiring in high dudgeon to Kilkenny. In Connaught they were more successful. Except for Galway which was occupied by Lord Clanricarde, the whole province was in the hands of the Irish. A party of Protestants had been attacked at Shrule, near Headford, and obliterated. When Clanricarde tried to bargain with the rebels for the lives of the remaining Protestants he was ordered by Parsons to desist. Before long not a man in Connaught outside Galway acknowledged any spiritual supremacy other than that of Rome.

By now in England Charles and his parliament were at loggerheads. They were agreed on the necessity of rapidly suppressing the Irish insurrection, but there gnawed into the minds of the parliamentary party the fear that the King, with a victorious army returned from Ireland, battle-hardened and gorged with the fruits of its prowess, might yet succeed with Strafford's policy. Vane's disclosures had led to the execution not only of the Viceroy, but also to any hope of reviving his policy. Parliament was prepared to vote in ample sufficiency the men, money and supplies needed for the Irish War; but they also insisted that the command of the army should be confided to their own nominee, whose orders, directives and instructions would come from them. Such a condition was unacceptable to the King; no army other than his could be permitted, for he would be at the mercy of any other. What sort of mercy could he expect from triumphant dissidents such as Pym, Vane, Hampden and the rest? Might they not reduce King Charles to a mere Mr Stuart? They would enforce their constitutional demands with zeal; and if they were resisted, with acerbity. Humiliation and indignity stared the King in the face; he refused to yield. The causes went far deeper, but the quarrel had developed which was to lead England into Civil War and the triumph of Cromwell. Each side demanded absolute control of the army, for in the last resort only the army could impose its will.

As the English sorted out their differences, there appeared in Ireland a central organization to direct the efforts of the Irish, the Kilkenny Confederacy.

The biographies of Wentworth already mentioned describe his last two years, often in graphic detail. His trial is to be found in:

J. Rushworth: *The Trial of Strafford.*

The State Trials, Vol. 3, pp. 1382 ff.

The Act of Attainder (16 Chas 1 c. 1) is reprinted in:

S. R. Gardiner: *Constitutional Documents*, pp. 156–158.

This work also contains the advice of the Twelve Peers, pp. 134; The Act for the Abolition of the Star Chamber, pp. 176–186; The Grand Remonstrance, pp. 202–232; and the King's Reply, pp. 233–236.

The story of the Rebellion of 1641 can be found in many works, amongst which may be mentioned:

E. Borlase: *History of the Execrable Irish Rebellion* (London, 1680).

J. A. Froude: *The English in Ireland* (London, 1881).

W. E. H. Lecky: *The English in Ireland in the 18th Century* (London, 1892).

R. Bagwell: *Ireland under the Stuarts.*

J. K. Hosmer: *Sir Henry Vane* (Samson Low, 1888).

W. W. Ireland: *Sir Henry Vane* (Nash, 1905).

CHAPTER 3
The Kilkenny Confederacy

THE year 1642 opened in England with a sense of impending doom. On 4 January King Charles entered the House of Commons with the intention of arresting the celebrated Five Members, but "the birds had flown". The failure of an act of violence invariably recoils upon the perpetrators, and this was no exception. In the King's humiliation his enemies made no attempt to conceal their delight. The Five Members had fled to the City of London where they appealed to the Lord Mayor for sanctuary. Their appeal did not fall on deaf ears, and the citizens of London resolved to face the roughs and bravoes upon whom the King depended. Communication between the King, now compelled to leave London, and his Parliament was reduced to formal letters, which became more acrimonious as time passed.

The two sides to the dispute formed their parties. The King attracted most of the nobility, the influence of the Church, the Catholics and those areas where reverence for the squire and the parson were still strong. Parliament rallied the new merchant classes, the City of London, the Dissenters and East Anglia. As the King wandered about the North Midlands and Yorkshire he was received with respect, and in some places with enthusiasm; but he could never obtain the overwhelming support to obliterate his opponents, nor could he provoke them into attacking him. He could neither fight without being branded as the aggressor, nor attack with the certainty of success.

The key to the situation lay in supplies. The King resolved to secure the control of the arsenals and the sea-ports through which they could be re-stocked; but he was beset by misfortune. Although Queen Henrietta Maria managed to send him a cargo of arms in July, his plans to seize the English fleet, lying in the Thames Estuary, went awry and the seamen remained obedient to parliament. In August the two Irish Sea guard frigates sided with parliament. The King now attempted to seize Hull where most of the arms and equipment saved from the disastrous struggle with Scotland were stored; but Sir John Hotham, the City Governor, backed by the townspeople, refused the King entrance. On 22 August, the King raised his standard at Nottingham, and the gage thrown down at Hull was taken up. The Great Civil War had started.

Meanwhile in Ireland the initial fury was spent. The only obedience was that given to the local strongman, and in the Catholic areas to the priesthood. At the beginning of March the bishops of Ulster met at Kells, where they declared that the rising was justified, that murder and usurpation of lands was not, and that it was the duty of all to fight for their religion, country and King. They knew that the English Parliament was their real enemy and that King Charles, already in grave difficulty, could not refuse their requests; by supporting the King they might even attract those Protestants who detested the stern discipline of the Puritans and the latest excesses of parliament. They knew that Ulster could not survive alone; to beat off the Scottish attacks they needed the aid of all Ireland. To obtain this they summoned a national synod of the whole Irish Church to meet at Kilkenny on 10 May 1642.

The synod at Kilkenny soon discussed secular matters, and the laity formed an association "to protect the King", to defend the power and privileges of the Parliament of Ireland, and to ensure the free exercise of the Catholic religion. A Supreme Council of twenty-four members was formed to provide an executive. Each province was to be governed by a provincial council of two members from each county, and each county was to have a council of two members from each barony. The Central Government, known as the General Assembly of the Confederate Catholics, was modelled on the Dublin Parliament with two orders; the upper order consisted of all the bishops, abbots and peers who were Catholics and would attend; the lower order comprised sixty-four county members and a hundred and sixty-two from the boroughs.

The Massacres of the Protestants, 1641

James Butler, 12th Earl and 1st Duke of Ormonde

The Supreme Council was to be chosen from the General Assembly and to be responsible to it. It was to have a guard of 500 foot and 200 horse; to supervise all inferior magistrates, to control the armed forces, and to act as the Supreme Court of the land. The arrangements took most of the summer, and then elections took place in the areas they controlled. The first elected assembly met in October. Lord Mountgarret became the President and Richard Bellings the Secretary.

By midsummer 1642 the Ulster Catholics lacked supplies and leadership. Their enemies were active and aggressive. The Anglo-Scottish forces now numbered over 12,000 men, and with a more thrusting commander, they ought to have exploited their advantage to put down the rising entirely. But then in July, unannounced, Owen Roe O'Neill arrived with 200 officers, trained and hardened in the service of France, three ship-loads of arms and ammunition, and two small English prizes he had managed to seize on his way from Flanders. He landed at Donegal where he was received with every sign of enthusiasm and joy. He made his way to Charlemont, which had been occupied by Lord Montgomery in June but abandoned after he had failed to reduce the rebel-held castle. Here O'Neill met the Ulster chiefs, who appointed him their Commander-in-Chief. He now commenced the difficult task of converting the gangs of the north into a disciplined force. The habits of outrage were infectious and difficult to eradicate; the supply system was non-existent; the need to provide against surprise was important; and it was vital to avoid a clash with the trained troops of General Munro. It is a measure of the capacity of O'Neill that he succeeded in training, disciplining and hardening his heterogeneous forces during the ensuing autumn and winter. By the spring of 1643 O'Neill was ready to lead his men into battle.

In Connaught Galway town was still held by the colonists, but the rest of the province was a waste where starving hordes wandered in search of food. In July 1642 Lord Ranelagh broke out of Athlone where he had been cooped up by the insurgents and marched to Ballintubber where he attacked O'Connor Don, the local chieftain. The discipline of the English made up for the inadequacy of their numbers and the absence of supplies. In spite of many and long sustained attacks the Irish were heavily defeated

5

and were fortunate indeed that the English supply situation prevented their turning the Irish retreat into a rout. In the following month some of the more irascible commanders of the English garrison in Galway, reinforced by Lord Forbes with seventeen ships, denounced the arrangements made with the local populace and began making armed and vicious forays into the neighbourhood. Satiated by their career of venom, these bands evacuated themselves by sea from this wilderness of their own making in September and descended upon Limerick.

In County Clare the Earl of Thomond, the local Protestant commander, had been unable to hold out against the Catholics and had left the scene. By midsummer 1642 the Catholics, under the command of Lord Muskerry and General Barry, consummated their success by capturing the fortress of Limerick with its guns, ammunition and supplies. Only the castle of Askeaton held out. In the rest of Munster the new President, Lord Inchiquin, saw that only by the very greatest exertions could he save himself after the fall of Limerick. When he asked Lord Forbes for help, he received none, and Forbes sailed away again to plunder the south coast of Ireland. However Inchiquin obtained assistance from the Boyle family, and by combing out the garrisons of Cork, Youghal and Kinsale, managed to raise an army of 1,600 men. With this small but determined and trained force he sought out the Irish forces at Liscarrol, some ten miles north-west of Mallow. Although the Irish had over 7,000 men, with the advantage both of artillery and a strongly entrenched position, Inchiquin drove them headlong from the field with great losses, but the absence of supplies prevented Inchiquin from following up his victory and he had to retire to Mallow where he was compelled to remain virtually inactive throughout the winter.

In Leinster the Marquis of Ormonde with the badly armed and ill-supplied English Army was subjected to the overriding control of two English parliamentary commissioners who were little interested in the King's service. Opposed to him were Lord Gormanstown and his brother Colonel Preston who commanded a growing Irish force whose discipline and training would soon bring to it a deserved superiority. Preston had learnt his trade in the religious quarrels of Germany and had landed in Wexford in September 1642 with substantial supplies, arms, ammunition and, above all, 500 trained and experienced officers whose zeal and capacity would convert the local Catholic levies into a formidable army.

Although, in accordance with the best concepts of ideal democracy the Kilkenny Confederacy was truly representative of the people, and was broadly based socially and geographically, the bad communications of Ireland prevented the representatives of the furthest regions, Ulster and Connaught, from regular attendance. This was a grave defect for Ulster had provided the leadership and all looked to Connaught for the provision of an inexhaustible supply of recruits. Insensibly the power of the Confederacy fell into the hands of the local landlords of Leinster and Munster who, although Catholics, were only half Irish and not anti-English. Provided there was no direct religious persecution they were not much interested in Milesian aspirations, as these represented a threat to themselves as much as to the English. Had not the old Irish been driven from the very land which they now occupied?

But above all, the crucial figure, the man who really held Ireland in the hollow of his hand, was Ormonde. A Protestant landlord with close Catholic connections, he was a devoted servant of King Charles and at the behest of his sovereign he would do as he was bidden, without hesitation and without any argument. He was a nephew of Lord Mountgarret and the brother-in-law of Lord Muskerry, one of the Kilkenny commanders in Munster. His family physician, Dr Fennel, was a member of the Supreme Council, and Kilkenny itself was a centre of Butler influence and power.

In the autumn of 1642 the Civil War in England erupted into major battles, as distinct from the squalid forays of the late summer. Once the harvest was in there was no reason for holding back, and the King set out for London. He passed through the Midlands, and on the road to Oxford at the end of October he met the Parliamentary Army at Edgehill. The fight which ensued was partially indecisive, but the King pushed on to enter Oxford in triumph a week later. After a short halt the Royal Army continued its march towards London, but after sacking Brentford they were confronted by a vastly superior force at Turnham Green, so they returned to Oxford for the winter. In January 1643, realizing that the Irish might turn the scales in his favour, King Charles instructed Ormonde and Clanricarde to enter into negotiations with the Kilkenny Confederacy. These instructions, secret though they were meant to be, dominated the scene in Ireland for many months to come.

Ormonde at first felt that he required some position of strength from which to negotiate. This coincided with the wishes of the Lords Justice to destroy any hopes of a settlement which would be inimical to English Parliamentary power and prestige. Borlase and Parsons therefore ordered Ormonde to attack Ross. In March 1643 he led his troops, some 3,000 strong, deep into Leinster and besieged the Irish garrison in Ross. The garrison, having been forewarned, was well prepared to resist. Soon Preston was gathering his forces and concentrating them with the intention of relieving Ross. Ormonde, having no intention of giving battle so far from help, raised the siege. As he marched back towards Dublin he was intercepted by Preston at Old Ross. Preston foolishly abandoned a strong position in a defile and was consequently badly beaten.

Negotiations were then begun between commissioners from the two sides at Trim on the 17 March. Neither side put much faith in the protestations of fidelity of the other; indeed it would be difficult to decide which side's sincerity was the more spurious. In June negotiations were broken off; but the incapacity to mount a full scale campaign to defeat the opposition caused them to be resumed fitfully, until in September 1643, a year's truce was arranged. The Pale was to be held by Protestant troops and most of the rest of the country was to be garrisoned by the Confederacy, who also agreed to raise a sum of £30,000 for the King's use. It was as well for the English connection that this truce had come into force, for the ability of the Dublin Government to withstand determined and protracted attacks by the Confederacy was highly dubious, as the staff of the army and the officials of the castle were split dangerously into the adherents of the King and the English Parliament. Disloyalty was rife, corruption had again become common, the army was badly fed, half-armed and mutinous and, in addition, the treasury was empty.

The Confederacy had steadily improved and sustained their authority in the rest of Ireland. Preston had been defeated in

March at Old Ross, but had managed to overwhelm the odd pockets of English resistance in central Ireland, capturing Ballinakill in April. In May Sir Charles Vavasour was badly defeated by Lords Muskerry and Castlehaven near Fermoy, losing 600 men with all baggage, cannon and ammunition. In June Burke captured Galway and all Connaught was in the hands of the Catholics. Ranelagh was compelled to abandon Athlone and had the greatest difficulty in making his way across eighty miles of hostile territory to Dublin. At the same time in Ulster, O'Neill was fortunate to escape capture by General Munro. Lords Montgomery and Moore carried out a sweep across Monaghan and Armagh driving the Catholics into Longford and Leitrim. Sir Robert Stewart, one of Munro's lieutenants, defeated a party of O'Neill's men near Clones, but the bulk of the Irish successfully escaped and were rapidly re-equipped, so that this incident had little effect on the main course of Ireland's history.

This period represented the high-water mark of the King's hopes and by a curious inversion the best chance of peace in Ireland. The negotiated truce had little effect on the marauding bands of the old Irish, and the terms were directly contrary to the wishes of the English parliamentary party, whose principal allies were the Scots of General Munro. In 1643 the Scottish Parliament had formally agreed to provide a contingent for Ireland in support of the English Parliament, and both agreed to exterminate the last remnants of the Catholic faith. In accordance with this, General Munro denounced the truce, signed the Solemn League and Covenant, and captured Belfast. The King had appointed Lord Portland, an English courtier who knew little about Ireland, to the post of President of Munster. Piqued by his own supersession, Inchiquin declared that he would thereafter support parliament. A few others followed his lead, but attempts to seize Dublin, Drogheda and Dundalk failed.

In January 1644 some Irish troops were sent to the King. They fared badly; one party of 150 was captured at sea and half of them were thrown overboard. Of those who landed safely the bulk were driven into Nantwich where 1,200 were taken prisoner and singled out for specially ignominious treatment. In spite of the severe consequences of quarrelling with the veterans of England, the Supreme Council knew that their only hope lay in their support of the King. But in the summer the Royalists had been defeated at Marston Moor, destroying the King's influence in the north and breaking his links with Scotland.

It was in the same year that Lord Maguire and Hugh MacMahon were brought to trial. After capture both had been subjected to intensive interrogation, and this probably included physical violence. Once this was over they were left in the dungeons of Dublin Castle for some months. In the middle of 1642 they were removed to the Tower of London. In August 1644, however, they escaped, but a month later they were seen by a servant of Sir John Clotworthy in Drury Lane and recaptured. In November they were arraigned in the Court of King's Bench for high treason. MacMahon was found guilty, sentenced to death and executed at Tyburn within a few days. Lord Maguire, however, pleaded his peerage; a long and involved argument delayed his trial, but it was held that a peerage in one country gave its holder no privilege in another. At these trials the whole grim story of the rising and its excesses was retold. To the mob of London the accused were the lowest form of parasite; its longing to witness the final scenes was gratified when Lord Maguire was hanged on 20 February 1645. To all the barbarity associated with a conviction for treason were added the insults inseparable from religious disorder and racial prejudice.

More grim news came to Ireland in 1645. In May the last great battle of the English Civil War was fought at Naseby when King Charles' last army was cut to pieces. A contingent of Irish infantry had joined the King just before the battle: they, their baggage train and their womenfolk were captured by Cromwell's horse and no mercy was shown. Of the women it was written, "about a hundred Irish ladies, not of quality, tattery camp-followers with long skean-knives about a foot in length which they well knew how to use; upon whom I fear the Ordinance against Papists pressed hard this day".

Naseby was the first victory of the Parliamentary Army after the "Self-Denying Ordinance", which had enabled parliament to cancel all army commissions granted for political reasons only. Only those officers whose records had been successful were re-commissioned, and these included General Cromwell. The consequences had already been largely anticipated; the "old decayed serving men, tapsters and such like" had been trained up to meet "gentlemen that have honour and courage and resolution in them", and they had been reinforced by "men of spirit". This was the army that was to sweep all before it in the next fifteen years; no foe would see its back; no fortress would withstand its storm; yet in the fullness of time it would sustain the restoration of the monarchy it had destroyed.

Early that year Charles had ordered Ormonde to convert the truce with Kilkenny into a permanent settlement; but nothing came of this. So at the end of August the Earl of Glamorgan went to Kilkenny and concluded a treaty with the Confederacy. By this the Catholics were to enjoy religious freedom, to hold those churches in Ireland actually in their hands, and to provide an army, 10,000 strong, for the King. The terms were to be kept secret until the army was ready. But in October the Catholic Archbishop of Tuam was killed in a skirmish near Sligo, and a copy of the treaty was found in his baggage. The secret was out, and it exposed the perfidy of the King once again.

Throughout these disorders French governments had watched the situation with mixed feelings. They were distressed at the humiliation of the Royalists, for the King's wife was both a Catholic and a French woman; but the internecine brawls of the English and the Irish removed any fears of an English irruption on to the Continent. At the worst the running sore of Ireland could be reopened to drain away England's strength; it became an essential part of French policy to keep the trouble simmering. At this time their policies in Italy were successful; the Pope was Urban VIII, a Florentine who had been the Papal Nuncio to France and was distinctly francophile. In the summer of 1643 Urban VIII sent Father Scarampi to Ireland to find out what was going on and to encourage the Catholic cause. When Scarampi passed through France Mazarin helped him on his way with arms and money. On arrival at Kilkenny Scarampi soon understood that what Ormonde said was just hot air, that the King was helpless, that the Supreme Council had no policy, that the Catholic forces were badly led and worse disciplined, and that the gentry were more interested in their estates than their religion. He urged the Confederacy to rectify their errors, to decide upon a policy and to ignore Ormonde. His reproofs served only to annoy his audience for the eternal bickerings and wild disorders continued. For two long years he struggled with the troubles of Kilkenny before he returned to Rome to report on his mission.

Suddenly the Supreme Council became alarmed. The defeat of King Charles at Naseby brought the dreadful prospect of a triumphant English Army before their eyes; even if they resolved their discords and disciplined their forces properly they could not hope to stand alone against the New Model Army. In desperation, Bellings was sent to Rome to appeal to the Church. A new Pope, Innocent X, the third Borgia to occupy the Vatican, was determined to provide the Irish with greater aid. As a fresh Papal Nuncio he appointed John Rinnuccini, Archbishop of Fermo.

Rinnuccini was then about fifty years old, strong-willed, very pious, and gifted with an acute and perspicacious mind. He was warned to have no truck with those timid Catholics who only wanted permission to practise their religion, for such was a right and to be publicly exercised; he was also warned about the various corruptions of Ireland. In the spring of 1654 Rinnuccini left Genoa; passing through Paris, he had a meeting with Cardinal Mazarin who provided him with a frigate to speed him on his way. The frigate, the *San Pietro*, left Ushant in the early autumn to be chased by an English frigate off Finisterre and only escaped capture by the onset of darkness. The envoy landed safely at Kenmare; with him travelled Bellings; with him, too, came plenty of arms, munitions and money. They crossed the mountains by Moll's Gap to Killarney, and a week later they reached Limerick. A further eighty miles brought them to Kilkenny. Cheering crowds lined the road all the way; all vied with each other in extending courtesies to the representative of the Roman Pontiff; a special Te Deum was sung to celebrate their safe arrival at Kilkenny. The merry-making now ended and Rinnuccini was brought face to face with the politics of the Confederacy.

Lord Mountgarret was old and vain; he was bitterly ashamed of himself for grovelling in front of Ormonde; he would not repeat the performance for an Italian, even if he were the Papal Nuncio. He suspected that his own behaviour was about to be subjected to impartial scrutiny: he was right. Rinnuccini knew that a policy of appeasement would be disastrous, and that his price for peace was beyond the comprehension of the Kilkenny prattlers. He soon appreciated the accuracy of Scarampi's reports, and he agreed with the measures recommended.

The cessation of active warfare and the non-enforcement of the penal laws had lifted a great load from the shoulders of the Catholic priesthood, but they were quite unprepared for this freedom. From being a hunted outcast, the parish priest had now become the virtual headman of the village, for which he was neither suited nor trained. Incompetence led to irregularities, and some forgot their sacred vows of poverty and chastity. The local autocracy of the squireen had been replaced by the authoritarian rule of the theocrat; the peasant did not notice the improvement.

By the end of 1645 the Puritan cause was almost extinguished in the south of Ireland. Rinnuccini was anxious that Dublin should be attacked before it could offer resistance. Ormonde, however, persuaded his agents to recall the General Assembly. It met in January 1646. The Nuncio, the clergy and the old Irish, divining the consequences of peace, were adamant for war: the nobility, more interested in consolidating their position, wanted peace. The latter view prevailed, and on 28 March a treaty was signed with Ormonde; by this the Confederacy were to provide the King with an army 10,000 strong in return for the repeal of the penal laws and a suspension of all further colonization. But it was too late. Chester, the King's last fortress, surrendered, and in May the King himself surrendered to the Scots. The provision of the Irish expeditionary force for service in England was no longer a viable proposition; but the same men would soon be needed urgently in Ireland.

In the spring of 1646 a fresh series of brawls and skirmishes erupted in the three southern provinces. Small parties of troops from both sides marched, generally unresisted, across the land, plundering and burning as they pleased. But in this quagmire the Nuncio saw the best destination for his gold. Ulster provided the main strength of the Puritan forces, where their communications with Scotland were safe; but also in the confines of Ulster lay the best-led Catholic Army in Ireland. These troops were little interested in money; their wants were few, and with true military virtue they preferred the cutting edge of their weapons to their personal comfort. Rinnuccini placed a third of his treasure at the disposal of Owen Roe. The immediate result was encouraging.

In May O'Neill's army was quartered in and around Cavan; it amounted to 5,000 infantry and 500 cavalry, well trained and eager to be led into battle. O'Neill was determined to fight such a battle as would give his men the long-delayed victory, as much to gratify their natural instincts as to gain for himself the pre-eminence among the Catholic generals to which his experience and skill entitled him. His position was strong, but two hostile armies lay seventy and a hundred miles away, at Sligo and beyond Belfast respectively. The weaker force had been driven into Sligo by General Preston. This western menace might have been removed by a rapid march and a swift battle; but if O'Neill left Cavan the way to the south would be open for Munro and his Scots. Robert Munro was at Carrickfergus with his main body, with his brother George on detachment at Coleraine and Stewart at Derry. At the beginning of June Munro realized that Preston was too far away to reinforce O'Neill if the latter were suddenly attacked, so he decided to concentrate his forces, bring O'Neill to battle at a disadvantage, defeat him, go on to ravage central Ireland, destroy the other forces of the Confederacy, and finally dictate terms to all Ireland. Ordering his brother and Stewart to meet him with all their strength on 5 June between Armagh and Monaghan, Robert Munro set off with 6,000 infantry, 600 cavalry, some guns and an abundance of supplies. Against such forces O'Neill had no chance, and his only course was to attack the largest single force and hope to defeat it before the concentration took place. He managed to occupy a position between the converging forces at Benburb on 4 June. Late that night he learnt that Munro after a long and weary march had entered Armagh, six miles away. Between the two armies lay the river Blackwater, a substantial obstacle which meandered down to Lough Neagh. It could be crossed by bridges at Moy, three miles downstream from Benburb, at Benburb itself, at Battleford where the Oona stream joins the river three miles above Benburb, and at Caledon, a further five miles upstream.

On the morning of 5 June Munro's army marched north-west from Armagh intending to cross the Blackwater at Battleford, but his advance guards found the bridge strongly held by O'Neill's picquets. In such a defile Munro could not deploy his strength, and he marched off to the south to cross unopposed at

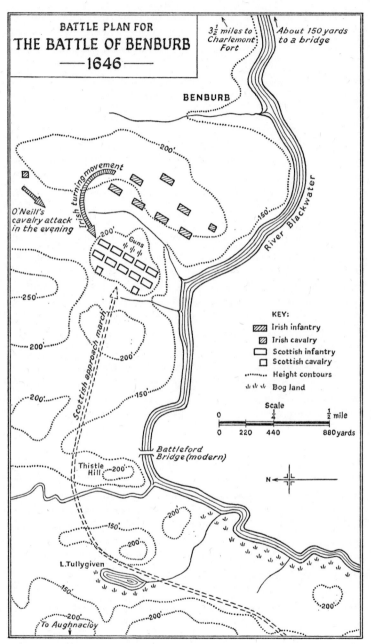

BATTLE PLAN FOR
THE BATTLE OF BENBURB
—1646—

3½ miles to Charlemont Fort

About 150 yards to a bridge

BENBURB

200'

Irish turning movement

O'Neill's cavalry attack in the evening

River Blackwater

150'

200'

Guns

250'

200'

200'

KEY:

Irish infantry
Irish cavalry
Scottish infantry
Scottish cavalry
Height contours
Bog land

Scottish approach march

200'

150'

Scale
¼

½ mile

0   220   440   880 yards

Battleford Bridge (modern)

Thistle Hill

200'

N

150'

200'

L.Tullygiven

150'

200'

200'

To Aughnacloy

200'

Caledon. O'Neill had been unable to reach this bridge before Munro, so he retired back towards the Oona stream, where he had already chosen a suitable spot to fight a defensive battle. Here his left would be protected by the swampy ground round the Oona, his right by a bog, while his centre occupied the only high ground in the neighbourhood. The position was such that cavalry could not be employed, and this enabled him to send his own horse to delay any advance by George Munro and Stewart who were expected to arrive from Dungannon at any moment. O'Neill drew up his troops facing a little east of south, so that until the late afternoon they would have the sun in their faces; this would not matter while it was high, but as the shadows lengthened towards evening it would be their assailants who would have the sun in their eyes.

Munro began by trying to turn the Irish left, and so weakened his own left. O'Neill took advantage of this by pushing his right forward, constricting Munro to the angle formed by the two rivers. Munro's artillery then started to bombard the Irish centre, but they were fairly well dispersed and little damage was done. By evening there was no sign of any result, but the Scots were on lower ground, could not manoeuvre, and had the sun in their faces. O'Neill's cavalry now returned after beating off George Munro's advance guard. O'Neill seized his chance. Throwing in every man who could stand, horse and foot alike, O'Neill charged the whole Scottish Army. The Scots thought the cavalry was their own and were taken at a major disadvantage. They rallied, however, and fought it out, but by nightfall half had been killed, and the rest retreated across the Blackwater leaving much of their stores, guns and baggage in the hands of the Irish. Neither side had given quarter, but about seventy wounded Scots were taken prisoner by the Irish in the morning. George Munro retired to Coleraine, while Robert was glad to halt at Lisburn to lick his wounds before going on to Carrickfergus. O'Neill then turned on Stewart, who had reached Augher in Tyrone, but when he heard of the Benburb disaster he retired in haste to Derry.

O'Neill now proceeded to throw away the richest prize which ever lay before Catholic Ireland. Munro's force in and around Carrickfergus amounted to barely 2,500 men, thoroughly shaken and unnerved. Assistance could not reach them from the north which was already menaced, nor from Sligo where Preston watched Sir Charles Coote. If O'Neill had attacked Munro again, the destruction of the Scottish forces would have been complete. Instead he moved supplies into Charlemont, which was in no danger, and then returned to Cavan, where he remained inactive for the next seven weeks.

The Supreme Council again began quarrelling over their future policy. Rinnuccini was confirmed in his belief that the Catholics could do without Ormonde and united could conquer the remaining Protestant parts of Ireland. But the party of Mountgarret were determined to make peace with Ormonde as the King's representative and at the end of July they succeeded. This infuriated O'Neill as his forces were now under the command of Ormonde. Rinnuccini was horrified. With nine bishops supporting him, he protested at the perfidy, pointing out that the peace did not guarantee the free and public exercise of the Catholic faith. When this protest was ineffective, he summoned a synod at Waterford; it promptly denounced the peace and excommunicated its authors. The synod was sustained by the opinions of the old Irish and by the major towns of the south.

O'Neill first thought of attacking Dublin after his victory at Benburb; but in view of the peace talks he was persuaded to wait. As he waited, reinforcements from England arrived in the Liffey. When he heard of the peace terms O'Neill's anger knew no bounds. Considering himself betrayed, he resolved to suppress the Supreme Council at Kilkenny; with 12,000 infantry and 1,500 cavalry, most of Munro's artillery and plenty of supplies, he had the means to do it. Early in August he left Cavan and marched rapidly southwards through West Meath, King's and Queen's counties to Roscrea, which he stormed; he then turned east and nearly captured Ormonde at Leighlinbridge; finally he halted outside Kilkenny. Here he was joined by Preston, who was only too glad to join the winning side. These two sent word to Rinnuccini at Waterford that the way was now clear, and at the end of September all three entered Kilkenny in triumph. The Supreme Council was dissolved with little ceremony, and a new one with Rinnuccini as President was formed.

The joint forces of O'Neill and Preston were now ready to

eliminate the central bastion of English influence, Dublin; the remaining fortresses would then fall like ripe plums. Once more jealousy prevented success. O'Neill advanced through Queen's County, where he left some garrisons, and on to Dublin. Preston found fault with this; why, he asked, had O'Neill frittered away his forces in garrisoning friendly towns? When Preston had passed through County Carlow, he had ignored the county town, which remained a standing menace in his rear. The two contingents met again nine miles from Dublin at Lucan, a village on the Liffey. O'Neill and Preston fixed their headquarters at Newcastle and Leixlip respectively. This was close enough for mutual support, and also for mutual quarrelling. Yet a swift and determined attack would have swept them into Dublin. The garrison was less than 6,000, and its defences were both weak in themselves and in very bad repair. But what Ormonde could not resist by strength, he would break up by guile. He began negotiations with Preston, the weaker character; then he sent Clanricarde to Leixlip with "fresh proposals". These came to nothing, but O'Neill found out and it effectively sowed distrust between him and Preston. O'Neill wondered if Preston and Ormonde might not join forces to fall upon him. Preston had much to gain and Ormonde as much to offer to make such a course attractive to both. The conviction that such treachery was possible grew until it was thought probable. At Christmas time O'Neill heard that parliamentary reinforcements had just entered Dublin; he waited no longer, but struck camp and retired into Queen's County. He was just in time, for Preston had been suborned by Ormonde to declare for peace and to serve under Clanricarde. The plot miscarried, and Preston was glad of Rinnuccini's efforts to reconcile him with O'Neill, but things were never the same again.

Preston was not the only victim of O'Neill's superior political sagacity. Athlone was held by Sir James Dillon, whose interests lay in the acquisition of Church lands; he wanted to be left alone to enjoy his ill-gotten gains. His position on the main road from Dublin to Galway at the crossing of the Shannon was one of great strength; it also formed a focal point for the collection of intelligence from all Ireland. He wanted to make peace with Ormonde. O'Neill heard of this and in January 1647 entered Athlone to deprive Dillon of his command. O'Neill had established himself in Maryborough, the modern Port Laoise, and from here he effectively controlled central Ireland.

In February 1647 another General Assembly was convoked at Kilkenny, but the disputes were now beyond composition, and the meetings were so disorderly that the expression "quarrelling like Kilkenny cats" has passed into the English language. But now a fresh force was appearing on the eastern horizon. The crafty policies of Ormonde in trying to play one side off against the other prompted him to permit the English parliamentary forces to land unopposed at Dundalk and Drogheda in the spring. The King had been handed over by the Scots to the English Parliament in return for payment for their troops in the Civil War. There was thus no real Royal party left, and Ormonde became the victim of the policies he had so often practised on others.

The parliamentary commander in Ireland was Michael Jones, an old veteran of the Civil War, brave, competent and well-fitted to the difficult task of saving what he could. By suggesting to Ormonde that the King would approve of the arrangement, Jones obtained possession of Dublin on 19 June. In accordance with the agreed terms the Royalists were guaranteed their lives and property, to go or stay in Dublin as they pleased. Ormonde received £5,000 in cash and a promise of a pension of £2,000 a year. He then went to England to tell the King about it all before going on to France.

The Pale was now in the hands of a well-disciplined and properly supplied force of about 5,000. The new commander ensured that within his enclave law and order prevailed. He was careful to pay for everything his troops needed, and to punish severely those breaches of discipline which affected the local population. These measures were immediately effective; the locals were anxious to trade on these terms, and the troops became a welcome contrast to their plundering and ravenous predecessors. At sea the Parliamentary Navy succoured their own and friendly forces, and intercepted such supplies as the Catholics could buy and ship. In Ulster Munro had recovered from his defeat, restored the morale and confidence of his men, and had reoccupied many of the positions hastily abandoned after Benburb.

In spite of the quarrels the Confederacy finally brought Preston's force up to a strength of 7,000 foot and 1,000 horse. He was

to attack Michael Jones in the Pale, and he hoped to get between
Jones and Dublin before surprising the city. Accordingly he laid
siege to Trim, which was held by a very small force. As soon as
Jones heard of Preston's movements he marched to the relief of
Trim. Catching Preston's covering force at a disadvantage at
Dungan's Hill, he defeated it, and then Preston's main body as it
came up to their support. Preston lost two-thirds of his men, all
his baggage and stores, and was fortunate to escape up the valley
of the Boyne. Jones had shown clearly that his men were far
superior to any Irish force so far encountered.

At the same time Inchiquin who had collected about 4,000
troops attacked and captured Cahir. He went on eleven miles to
Cashel, which lay at his mercy. He demanded £3,000 and offered
the garrison their lives if they surrendered the town. The terms
were rejected, and the garrison and townspeople retired on to
the Rock of Cashel, a three hundred and fifty foot outcrop of
hardened limestone which dominates the local countryside.
Furious at being denied their booty, Inchiquin's troops assaulted
the Rock. After a long and arduous battle they finally broke
through the Irish lines to cut the garrison to pieces, to desecrate
the local shrines, and to gorge themselves on such plunder as they
could find. This massacre goaded Lord Taafe, a local Confederate
commander, to action.

Learning that Inchiquin had marched off south-westwards,
Taafe followed him to Mallow. Just beyond the town the two
forces met at Knockanoss. Taafe's right wing was commanded
by Alasdair Macdonald, a wild Ulsterman and the former commander of Montrose's Irish in Scotland. Macdonald, "no sojer
but stout enough", began the action with the type of wild charge
he had learnt to deliver in Scotland; brilliantly successful, it drove
Inchiquin's left in rout from the field. Inchiquin retaliated by
attacking Taafe's left and centre; this, too, was successful and
the defeated Irish fell back in disorder. Inchiquin now turned
to catch Macdonald's men returning in disarray after their wild
chase; they, Montrose's lieutenant among them, were all cut to
pieces.

The only army now left to the Confederates was that of O'Neill.
When O'Neill heard of Knockanoss he was at Boyle in Roscommon preparing to attack Sir Charles Coote in Sligo. He had

to abandon this enterprise to re-cross Ireland to stand between Kilkenny and Michael Jones, who was preparing to join Inchiquin and finish off the Confederacy. To increase his field force, Jones stripped the garrisons of Trim and Naas; O'Neill promptly occupied Trim. The previous successes of Jones and his habit of paying for supplies had generated prosperity in the Pale. The Irish needed little encouragement to forage in such pastures, and O'Neill sent out raiding parties from Trim to probe towards Dublin and to deny the English local supplies. O'Neill alone kept Jones in Dublin; he refused to be brought to battle, and thus kept his force intact. Yet this drove the Confederacy frantic; they did not understand Fabian policies. Rather than sustain such a commander as O'Neill, they negotiated a cession of arms with Inchiquin in April 1648.

A lesser man than O'Neill might have given up in despair. The squabbling gentry of Kilkenny were not worth fighting for, and had they been abandoned they would have had themselves to blame. They had neither made peace nor waged war. They richly deserved what they ultimately got, and the pity of it was that they did not get it sooner. On learning of the cessation O'Neill denounced it; so did Rinnuccini, who made his way to O'Neill's camp at Maryborough and told the clergy to preach against "this pestilential peace". The Supreme Council denounced the Nuncio and declared O'Neill a rebel! O'Neill promptly struck camp at Trim and marched southwards; avoiding Inchiquin he threatened Kilkenny by ravaging the countryside; and finally he returned to re-establish himself at Belturbet, only eleven miles from his original base at Cavan, in the late summer of 1648. The Supreme Council continued to fulminate against him, but the best Catholic general in Ireland ignored their fury, which he rightly regarded as akin to that of a thwarted and spoilt brat.

In the spring of 1648 Ormonde reported to the Queen in Paris. During discussions with her and with other Irish notables Ormonde agreed to resume his old duties as Lord Lieutenant. He was influenced by Cardinal Mazarin's blessing and liberal promises, by the plot to re-open the English Civil War which he thought had a good chance of success, and by Inchiquin's dissatisfaction with the rewards to him for his services to the English Parliament. But when the Second Civil War broke out the Scottish

Royalists suffered a crushing defeat at Preston, and the survivors were glad to shelter behind the rearguard formed by Munro who had crossed from Ulster to support the rising. By the autumn it was known that King Charles was being kept in close confinement on the Isle of Wight. It was time for Ormonde to leave for Ireland, and at the end of September he reached Kilkenny. He had no time to waste, and his energy was remarkable. In reply to an address of welcome he dissolved the Confederacy, but promised that their work would be remembered. He also promised religious freedom, and that Ireland would be governed by Irishmen; yet he declared Rinnuccini a rebel and arrested his assistant, the Dean of Fermo. The Archbishop fled to Galway where he was besieged by Clanricarde. After he was certain he could do no more good in Ireland, and in spite of the pleadings of O'Neill, the Nuncio sailed away in January 1649. His mission had been heartbreaking; he had seen so many missed opportunities, and often the ultimate prize had been within Ireland's grasp; he had been horrified at the mutual vituperation of Catholic Irishmen, and he had tried unsuccessfully to assuage their bitter hatreds. All he could take away was the knowledge that where he had failed no one else could have done half as well.

A storm was about to break; to meet it Ormonde needed the unflinching loyalty of every Irishman, Catholic and Protestant alike. He intended to acquire the support of such diverse characters as O'Neill, Inchiquin, Preston and Munro; and they had to bring their troops with them. He invited the old Confederates to nominate twelve of their number to assist him in the government. These nominees, known as the Commissioners of Trust, included Lords Dillon and Muskerry. He also appealed to Jones and Coote, telling them that he was deceiving the Catholics in order to make them fight; but Jones and Coote ignored him. He judged Inchiquin by the same standards; the President of Munster had turned his coat once, and might do so again. He was not to be trusted!

Munro and his fellow Scots who had escaped from the debacle at Preston were appalled on their return to Ireland to hear of the sufferings of King Charles. Stupid and foolish, even faithless, he may have been, but he was still a Scot. They would cease to quarrel with his representative in Ireland. The cessation of hostility by the Ulster Scots was good for Ormonde, for it also stopped the desultory fighting in Southern Ulster, and opened up a route to the King's friends in Scotland.

Only O'Neill's views were unknown; he did not trust Ormonde and the departure of Rinnuccini had been painful. He would not fight his co-religionists, but he dreaded any Protestant alliance. He decided to wait. With the best disciplined Catholic force in Ireland, with a long record of success against powerful enemies, the side he ultimately supported would probably give him substantial guarantees for the future and liberal conditions in the meantime. O'Neill's views were also those of the major towns. It is hard to criticize such an attitude, for in the shifting quicksands of Ireland yesterday's friend would be tomorrow's enemy; the dissipation of one's strength in futile marches and expeditions was the sure way to disaster. But during this period of waiting, when his weight could have tipped the scales either way, the opportunity was missed, and after this it was too late.

In the autumn of 1648 Munro and Stewart were surprised and taken prisoner in Belfast and Derry respectively. The loss of these two garrisons and their commanders was a serious blow to Ormonde. Another blow was his failure to attract Lord Broghill, the Boyle commander in Youghal. His waiting game was based on the further acquisition of land, and to do this he had to be certain of who would be the ultimate victor!

After the execution of King Charles it was believed in the early spring of 1649 that the Prince of Wales would come to Ireland in person; this might have decided the important waverers like O'Neill. Indeed the King's cousin, the celebrated Prince Rupert of the Rhine, brought a squadron of the reconstituted Royal fleet to the Munster ports. But the Irish did not comprehend the value of sea power, nor did Rupert enlighten them in this respect. The Irish were bitterly disappointed that Rupert's ships had not brought them men, arms and money; yet these selfsame ships provided the means, by way of blockade, of reducing the remaining Parliamentary garrisons. For want of this simple understanding, the Royal fleet lay idle in harbour until in July Parliamentary frigates threatened to blockade them in their turn and they were glad to escape to Portugal.

In spite of these failures and difficulties Ormonde began campaigning in April 1649. The first ray of hope came from Enniskillen, where the people proclaimed Charles II King. The garrison had refused to dissipate its strength or to provoke powerful enemies by forlorn enterprises; by their courage and wisdom they infused some enthusiasm into themselves and their neighbours. In May Lord Castlehaven, operating in central Ireland, occupied Maryborough where he managed to persuade O'Neill's men to accept Ormonde's authority; but again the best news was from the north. Munro had escaped; he resumed the command of his Scots, and in addition he obtained an order from King Charles II to co-operate with Ormonde. Munro arranged with Clanricarde to attack Sligo; the two commanders crossed Ulster and Connaught respectively and fell upon the town from north and south at the same time. The campaign was a model of strategic and tactical surprise, and Sligo fell with hardly any fighting. George Monck, the parliamentary commander in Ulster, then abandoned Lisburn and withdrew into Dundalk and Drogheda. The parliamentary forces everywhere were now experiencing distress; they lacked food and ammunition; they were short of funds, and were being wasted by desertion, disease and disorder.

It was now that Ormonde had a chance to seize Dublin. In June he and Inchiquin arrived at Finglas, three miles from Dublin, with substantial forces. But they were shocked to learn that Monck and O'Neill had agreed to a local truce; this meant that Ormonde's rear was only a day's march from a hostile force, and an assault on Dublin would be courting disaster. Inchiquin was accordingly sent with 2,000 infantry and 1,500 cavalry to eliminate this danger. He captured Drogheda with little trouble, and Trim fell shortly afterwards; in July he moved on to Dundalk. Here Monck had an abundance of supplies but an inadequate garrison; forty miles away at Clones, O'Neill had plenty of men but no ammunition. The two commanders agreed to rectify the position. Accordingly O'Neill advanced with a substantial force to Cullaville, a small village about seven miles from Dundalk. From here he sent General Farrell with 500 foot, 300 horse and a train of waggons into Dundalk for the ammunition. Inchiquin learnt of what was happening, and as the waggons returned, he attacked the convoy with all his strength. His men cut the escort to bits and seized the ammunition. As a result Monck still had not got the men, nor O'Neill the powder. The former was compelled to surrender, the latter to retreat. Newry and Carlingford were also occupied by Inchiquin, who then allowed Monck to return to England. Although Coote in Derry was in acute distress, Inchiquin left him alone and returned in high spirits to Finglas.

But while Inchiquin had been away, a parliamentary convoy had arrived in the Liffey, bringing a reinforcement of 2,000 Ironsides, all veterans of the Civil War and the advance guard of the armament now preparing in England for the reconquest of Ireland, an abundance of supplies and, above all, reassurance to the starving and disheartened garrison that relief was at hand. To Ormonde it was now or never. But he was still afraid of a parliamentary landing in the south, and he again committed the military sin of dispersing his forces before battle. He sent Inchiquin with his victorious troops back to Munster to act as a deterrent to a landing there and to function as a general reserve. For the latter purpose even a day's march would be too far away, while for 3,500 men to cover a coastline of 200 miles was absurd. At the critical moment when these very troops might have tipped the scales they were not available.

In 1649 Dublin was a very small town compared with the modern city. It was bounded on the north by the river Liffey; on the east the wide space of College Green separated the city from Trinity College; on the south and west a wide arc carried the boundary past the Castle to the modern Usher's Quay. The road to the north crossed the Liffey just south of St Michan's Church where the Four Courts now stand; a mile and a half to the north of this the road forked to cross the Folka stream at Finglas and Glasnevin. The road to the west ran along the south bank of the Liffey, past Kilmainham and the Phoenix Park; but a considerable complex of routes came in from the south. The most westerly of these came from Terenure, through Rathfarnham, past Harold's Cross to enter the city just south of the Liffey bridge; the next came from Rathmines; the third and fourth came from Bray and Kingstown (the modern Dun Laoghaire) to converge on St Stephen's Green before entering the city beside the Castle.

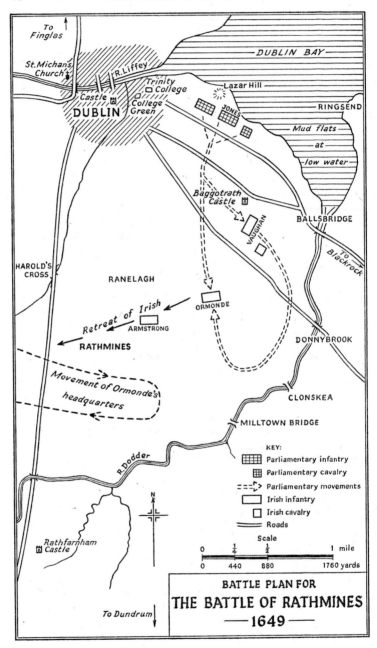

To Finglas

St. Michan's Church

R. Liffey

Castle

DUBLIN

Trinity College

College Green

DUBLIN BAY

Lazar Hill

JONES

RINGSEND

Mud flats

at

low water

Baggotrath Castle

VAUGHAN

BALLSBRIDGE

To Blackrock

HAROLD'S CROSS

RANELAGH

ORMONDE

Retreat of Irish

ARMSTRONG

RATHMINES

DONNYBROOK

Movement of Ormonde's headquarters

CLONSKEA

MILLTOWN BRIDGE

R. Dodder

KEY:

▦ Parliamentary infantry

▦ Parliamentary cavalry

- - -▷ Parliamentary movements

▭ Irish infantry

□ Irish cavalry

═ Roads

N

Rathfarnham Castle

Scale

0   ¼   ½   1 mile

0   440   880   1760 yards

BATTLE PLAN FOR
THE BATTLE OF RATHMINES
—— 1649 ——

To Dundrum

Ormonde intended to use the easier access from the south in his attack on Dublin; he wished to begin by cutting the city off from the sea by fortifying some high ground adjacent to the river known as Lazar Hill. Accordingly he left Lord Dillon with 2,500 men in Finglas with orders to blockade the road to the north; with the remainder he marched in a wide sweep to the west of Phoenix Park, crossed the Liffey and swept down on Rathfarnham. He captured the small English garrison there, and continued his march through Rathmines to Baggotrath, a strong, stone-built outpost about a mile from the Castle on the Kingstown road where Lower Mount Street now crosses the Grand Canal. Ormonde seized this and began the works necessary to safeguard his plan. Jones appreciated the importance of Ormonde's moves, and noted the loss of grazing for his cavalry by the occupation of the fields south of the city. He decided to attack with all his strength. On 2 August he advanced along the water's edge down the Liffey to attack Sir William Vaughan near the mouth of the river Dodder. Sir William was killed, and his troops driven off. Jones now went on to attack Ormonde's centre; he recaptured Baggotrath and only just failed to capture Ormonde himself. Sir Thomas Armstrong, commanding Ormonde's left, arrived with 1,000 cavalry just in time to cover the retreating Irish and prevent their discomfiture becoming a rout; but Ormonde lost his ammunition reserves, much equipment and about £4,000 in gold. Taafe tried to persuade Dillon to enter Dublin from its unprotected north, but Dillon would take no risks, even if such a bold and unpredictable action had every prospect of success. With the rest of Ormonde's battered army, Taafe and Dillon retired to Trim and Drogheda.

Michael Jones could now look at Ireland with a much less jaundiced eye. His troops had just defeated the largest army in the country; Dublin was safe; he had been reinforced and supplied on a generous scale; and he knew that one of the greatest armies of all time would soon come to complete his work. For Ormonde the outlook was bleak, but the disaster at Rathmines was nothing compared to the crushing defeats which were to follow.

The Kilkenny Confederacy is well described both by Bagwell and Borlase.
Rinnuccini's mission has been described in his correspondence published
under the title of *The Embassy in Ireland* (Dublin, 1873).
The Trial of Lord Maguire can be studied in the *State Trials*, Vol. 4, p. 654.
The "mercy" shown to the Irish women comes from J. Whitlocke, reprinted in
Carlyle's *Letters and Speeches of Oliver Cromwell*.
As before, Gardiner's *Constitutional Documents* provide a mine of original
documents, including The Self-Denying Ordinance, pp. 287–288.
See also:

J. C. Beckett: *The Making of Modern Ireland, 1603–1923* (Faber and Faber, 1966).

J. T. Gilbert: *Contemporary History of Affairs in Ireland* (1880).

T. L. Coonan: *The Irish Catholic Confederacy and the Puritan Revolution* (1956).

CHAPTER 4

The Preparation of the Expedition

THE axe flashed in the wintry sunlight; the King was dead.

On 30 January 1649 Charles I was beheaded outside his palace in Whitehall. That day the ordinary soldier might have been excused if he thought that his work was done. He had served Parliament in a fashion that had given him an intense feeling of pride in himself. No enemy, Royalist or Scot, had seen his back. He knew no outcome of battle other than victory. He had fought for a cause in which he passionately believed, and that cause had triumphed. He was "no idle tapster"; he was one of the Lord's annointed, chosen to lead the nation out of bondage, and now the nation was the master of its own destiny, or rather the soldier was. His fury at the faithlessness of Charles Stuart was assuaged; the man was dead, his wife an exile, his son a fugitive, and his adherents defeated, dispersed and despoiled. The soldier could now bear home his trophies in triumph, beat his sword into a ploughshare, and make his spear a reaping hook. But eleven more years, years in which his country would rise from a brawling backwater to be the dominant power in Europe, were to pass before his service was to end, and to end in his acceptance of Charles, Prince of Wales, as King.

The leaders of the army, and Cromwell in particular, had long regarded the news from Ireland with disgust. Now that the Civil War was over, they were determined to settle accounts with these turbulent people. The stern Puritan himself would lead his devoted Ironsides to Ireland and reduce that country to obedience. To this martinet there was only one punishment for rank insubordination, and he would inflict it. The day of battle would show God's wishes, and God's will would be done by the soldiers. After the battle, they would complete the task.

Once the King had been executed the parliamentary party leaders had numerous high constitutional problems to solve. To the Royalists, the Scots, the Irish and Europe, the Prince of Wales was now King Charles II: but this thought was quite intolerable to the victors. The same afternoon that the King had been beheaded the House of Commons declared that the proclamation of his son as King would be treated as treason.

It was also necessary to appoint a supreme executive authority in the State. A fortnight later, on 13 February 1649, the House resolved to set up a Council of State. It was made up of John Bradshaw, President of the Court which had tried the King, Generals Fairfax and Cromwell, the younger Vane and thirty-seven others. Its tasks were the suppression of any Royalist revolt, the supreme command of the army, the conduct of foreign affairs, the administration of the revenue, and the use "of all good ways and means for the reducing of Ireland . . . and . . . the securing, advancement and encouragement of the trade of England and Ireland".

On Tuesday 13 March this Council began discussing the question of Ireland. The first task was to nominate the new Commander-in-Chief of their expeditionary force. Towering above all other candidates for this post was Oliver Cromwell, and he was proposed for it by Fairfax. Two days later he accepted. At the same time John Milton, the poet, was appointed the Secretary to the Council.

The new Commander-in-Chief was born in 1599, a great-nephew of Thomas Cromwell, Henry VIII's Vicar-General, who had superintended the suppression of the monasteries sixty years previously. His family came from the rising middle class, somewhat awed by the militant anti-clerical destruction of the Reformation and anxious to propitiate Fate by a devout Faith, and a concomitant determination to prosper and do well in the world. His father, Robert, was a younger son of a local landowner, so he obtained his living from the soil and the fattening of livestock; it is said that his income was £300 a year, a substantial fortune in those days. Oliver's youth was spent in and around Huntingdon.

During the period of the King's Personal Rule, the Cromwells had been affronted by the arrogance of Royal presumptions, but like most of their countrymen they were not averse to making money out of the placid and prosperous state of the country. The small fortune thus acquired enabled Oliver to buy some debentures on Irish land in 1642.

In King Charles's third parliament Cromwell represented Huntingdon; but in both the Short and the Long Parliaments he had sat for Cambridge Town. Although he had the appearance of an unsophisticated countryman, it was not long before "he was very much hearkened unto"; in spite of an "untuneable" voice, he rose steadily in the ranks of the parliamentary party. At the outbreak of the Civil War he had ensured the adhesion of Cambridge to Parliament by seizing the local supplies of arms. In the years that followed, his command rose from that of a cavalry regiment to the whole Parliamentary Army. A strict disciplinarian, he also had that rare gift of seeing and seizing military opportunities. He was over forty when the Civil War began and had no previous experience in warfare whatsoever; yet in two years he had made his name, and in another the world knew that a military genius had appeared on English fields. At the same time Oliver was improving himself in debate, diplomacy and negotiation. Once the fighting in England ended Oliver took his part in seeking a final settlement; it was only when this came to nothing that he gave up in disgust. When the King saw fit to stir up a second Civil War, Cromwell fell in with his brother officers' opinion that the King had forfeited his right to live. Oliver played out his part, and we may see to this day his firm bold signature on the formal Death-Warrant. His actions and motives on this occasion will be argued till the end of time; his brother officers knew that thereafter there could be no turning back, for him or them.

The problems which beset the new Commander-in-Chief were important. He had to measure the real strength of the Irish forces, so that he could decide the numbers he would require for his Expeditionary Force; he had then to raise, equip, pay and move this army; to provide for its maintenance and to arrange its passage to Ireland; and finally to ensure that after arrival there its training and equipment would guarantee a rapid and total victory.

Cromwell was well aware of Ormonde's advantages and weaknesses. He was well provided with up-to-date intelligence about Ireland; his key positions in Dublin and the Pale enabled reports to be collated and cross-checked prior to transmission across the Irish Sea. With the aid of similar reports from the south, Cromwell knew the necessity of attacking Ormonde before he had time to consolidate his position, and knew that a serious defeat would help in disintegrating the Irish forces; once defections had started Cromwell felt reasonably certain of ultimate success.

Cromwell knew that Inchiquin was a worthless specimen; he was well aware of Lord Thomond's influence around Bunratty; he was aware of Owen Roe O'Neill's dissatisfaction with the Kilkenny Confederacy and he approved of refusals to sell him even a fleeting immunity, for he had shared in the exploitation of the initial rising: "the innocent blood which had been shed in Ireland was too fresh in their memory, and that House (of Commons) did detest and abhor the thought of closing with any party of Popish rebels." If O'Neill could be driven back on Ormonde, these two would almost certainly quarrel. In the north, the Scots still smarted from the execution of the King; but they also smarted from the defeat at Benburb; and religious differences would serve to introduce discord between them and Ormonde. But above all, Cromwell knew that Ormonde could never concentrate his forces for battle; they were forever dispersed. But, because he had command of the sea, Cromwell could land his punch where he pleased. With naval escorts the Ironsides could land anywhere, re-embark if necessary, and then land somewhere else; and all the time they would have supplies, reinforcements and transport. On this basis, therefore, Cromwell decided on a force of 8,000 infantry, 3,000 light cavalry, 1,200 dragoons and eight field guns.

In the provision of men for the expedition Cromwell found many serious difficulties, particularly in the problems of pay and propaganda. Already the pay of the army was badly in arrears, raising the further problems of pillage and desertion. Parliament had been singularly fortunate in the past in being able to raise substantial sums of money, both by taxation and by borrowing, in order to pay their army. At that time the infantryman received ninepence per day, the dragoon one shilling and ninepence, and the light cavalryman two shillings and three pence, but they had to maintain their horses out of this stipend. Officers naturally were paid more: infantry majors drew thirteen shillings, and cavalry subalterns five shillings and fourpence per day; both were also granted an allowance of two shillings a day for each horse. It is always difficult to equate such payments to the scales of today, since commodity prices have changed both directly and in relation to each other; nevertheless some concept of the real value of the soldier's pay may be obtained from the general price of wheat at this period of sixty-five shillings and sixpence per quarter, and the average wage for agricultural labourers was about eightpence per day. The private soldier was not well paid, but his officers were, and cavalrymen were in a better position than infantrymen. The whole army required an annual budget of £1,500,000, which included the cost of the various services, the provision of ammunition, stores and equipment. Cromwell considered his force would require about half this sum annually. Feeling that it would be undesirable and foolish to move without a substantial treasure chest, he refused to embark upon his campaign until £100,000 had been paid to him in cash. He knew that he could only pay his troops, the contractors and for services in Ireland in specie; it was well appreciated there that "promises to pay" were as worthless as the paper on which they were written. His prudence in this respect was to have far-reaching effects; he could enforce a very strict discipline on his troops; he was to create the conditions under which the Irish peasant would be paid for his labour (a fresh departure in the Emerald Isle); and he was to provide a basis of integrity upon which a fresh settlement might be founded.

The effects of the propaganda were more subtle. The consequences of the Reformation had produced among Protestants a wide range of doctrines based on different interpretations of some vague and ephemeral sentence somewhere in Holy Writ; none of the classical heresies was without its equivalent in the England of the early Stuarts. The very wildest of notions were carried into the parliamentary camp. In a laudable attempt to maintain the morality and zeal of the troops in 1647 Parliament had appointed "Army Adjutators"; these were the militant Puritan preachers, and they depended for their influence upon the vigour with which they expounded their doctrines. They had proclaimed that with

"Justice upon the King" and the establishment of a free commonwealth, the Millenium would come, with life a bed of roses. When'
their predictions were not fulfilled discontent, and later disobedience, became rife. Cromwell was gravely embarrassed by
this, for it was upon these enthusiasts that he depended to whip
up the zeal of his men to avenge the innocent blood shed in
Ireland.

At the beginning of April the Army Council met to decide which
regiments should be earmarked for Ireland. After prayers they
decided to pick the units by lot. Tickets were made out, put into
a hat, and drawn out by a child; fourteen infantry and fourteen
cavalry regiments were chosen in this manner. The officers of the
twenty-eight were delighted; it meant that they would continue
in well-paid employment, and there would be an opportunity to
obtain an Irish estate on which they and their families might
settle. But the rank and file felt otherwise; they wanted their
discharge and the privilege of going home; their work was done,
and why should not Ireland stew in its own juice? And what about
their arrears of pay? There was trouble within a week.

Whalley's regiment was quartered in the City of London. They
were not required for Ireland, but their accommodation was
needed for the assembly of those who were, so they were ordered
to leave. One troop seized its commander in the Bull Inn at
Bishopsgate , and they refused to move until their grievances had
been redressed. Fairfax and Cromwell immediately went to the
Bull, quelled the mutiny, sent the troop off to their new quarters,
and seized fifteen men who were instantly tried by court-martial.
Five were found guilty and sentenced to death; but only one, a
Trooper Lockyer, was actually shot, outside St Paul's Cathedral.
This did not stop the trouble, for sympathizers with Lockyer
chose to wear sea-green ribbons in their hats and this habit
spread to the troops.

On 9 May Cromwell reviewed the London contingent for Ireland in Hyde Park. Some of the men were wearing these sea-green
ribbons. With a mixture of cajolery and force he eliminated these
mutinous emblems and delivered an address as much for the
world at large as for the troops themselves. He referred to the
successes of Parliament, the returning signs of prosperity, the
punishment of the Royalists with heavy fines to pay the troops'

wages and the other tranquillizing measures. He roundly abused those who could not endure hardship and offered those who wished it their discharge, but without any promise of their arrears of pay. The troops were only quietened by this; they were not really satisfied and were far from being cowed.

Cromwell was now alarmed to hear of other mutinous acts across the south of England where the Expeditionary Force was assembling. At Banbury a Captain Thompson with 200 men refused to obey orders; his Colonel attacked at once and dispersed the mutineers. Thompson fled towards Northampton, but was cornered in a wood and killed. His brother, a Cornet in Salisbury, brought out over 1,000 in sympathy and left to join the Banbury men. Fairfax and Cromwell set out immediately to suppress this outburst. Covering 50 miles a day they surprised the mutineers at Burford on 15 May; the surprise was so great that there was no resistance and the rising collapsed. A court-martial was immediately assembled and the ringleaders tried. Cornet Thompson and two corporals were shot on 17 May in the churchyard at Burford in the presence of their comrades; the remainder were then reprieved. The dissidents, happy to escape with their lives, were marched off to Devizes and then dispersed to different regiments to serve in Ireland. Fairfax and Cromwell then entered Oxford for a few days rest before returning to London. All was now quiet; discipline had been restored, and the remaining preparations went swiftly forward.

After his return to London Cromwell arranged to pay off some, but not all, of the arrears of his troops. He also renewed the offer he had made in Hyde Park to the whole army: any man could have his discharge, the price of which was the total sum standing to his credit. This was the economic philosophy of the carrot and the stick; either prosperity and plenty in the future, or nothing. If the troops were successful, the promise could be redeemed; if they were not, it would not matter: but this pie in the sky was within their reach. Cromwell, too, could appeal to the patriotism and cupidity of his men in the same breath.

On 10 July the new Lord Lieutenant of Ireland (for Cromwell had been appointed to this office as well) left London in his coach, a cumbrous waggon requiring six Flanders mares to draw it. He was accompanied by his staff, a lifeguard of eighty horse, and a large retinue of servants. The next day was a Sunday, and the great cavalcade halted for divine service: "three ministers did pray and the Lord Lieutenant himself and Colonel Goffe and Colonel Harrison did expound some places of scripture excellently well and pertinent to the occasion." Four days later they reached Bristol, where they stayed for a fortnight before going on to Milford Haven. Here on 13 August he embarked on the *John*, which sailed on the tide with a fair wind for Ireland.

Meanwhile Ironside regiments had been marching across England and Wales for the embarkation ports. Their morale was high for they had been paid; and the enthusiasm of the people for the settling of accounts with Ireland was not unmixed with pleasure at witnessing the departure of such terrible masters. The weather was fine that summer, and the organization of the move was neither upset by gale force winds nor hindered by heavy rain. Cromwell intended to use his sea power so that only at the last minute need he make a decision about where he would land, although it would be in the south. Accordingly his transports were assembled in the Welsh ports, and these were a scene of bustle and activity.

Before following the Ironside fortunes in Ireland it is necessary to examine their organization, equipment, discipline and supply system, because it was on these cornerstones that Cromwell was to found his martial philosophy and his great victories. On these foundations, too, he bequeathed to his Royal successors a force which the leading nations of Europe were only too anxious to find aligned with their own.

A cavalry regiment consisted of six troops, each of four officers and one hundred troopers. The commanding officer was a lieutenant-colonel with a major as his second-in-command; each was also a troop commander. The troop officers were a captain, a lieutenant, a cornet and a quartermaster; the field officers' troops were virtually commanded by their lieutenants, and the colonel's subaltern was known as a captain-lieutenant; he was generally considered to have the right to the first vacancy as a troop commander.

An infantry regiment comprised ten companies, but these were of different sizes: the colonel's company numbered two hundred, the lieutenant-colonel's one hundred and sixty, the major's one hundred and forty, and the rest one hundred each. The officers of a foot company consisted of a captain, a lieutenant and an ensign; as in the cavalry the colonel's subaltern was known as a captain-lieutenant. The non-commissioned officers were two sergeants, three corporals and a gentleman-at-arms, a store-keeper responsible for the preservation, repair, marking and issue of all arms and ammunition.

The artillery ordered for the Irish expedition was approved by the Council of State on 17 July 1649 when they issued a warrant for Captain Edward Tomlins, the comptroller of Cromwell's artillery, to draw two eight-inch cannon, two seven-inch cannon, two demi-cannon, two twenty-four pounders, three culverins, two demi-culverins and ten sakers. The Piece of Eight, or the eight-inch cannon, fired a sixty-four pound shot and was quite accurate for ranges up to 400 yards; it had an extreme range of about $1\frac{1}{2}$ miles, and required a team of ten oxen to drag it along the appalling roads of those days. Its narrow, solid tyres dug deep ruts in the road, making its employment in conditions of mobile warfare almost impossible. The demi-culverin was a much more serviceable weapon, firing a shot of 12 pounds accurately about 350 yards; it had an extreme range of 2,000 yards, and only required six horses to draw it. Sakers, minions and drakes were smaller, firing balls of six, four and three pounds respectively, and not requiring more than four horses to draw them; their range was short, but their rate of fire was usually about one round every four minutes compared with six minutes for the big guns. All these guns were muzzle-loaded, and were fired by a train of powder through a touch-hole. The propellant was invariably gunpowder, which was manufactured very crudely from saltpetre in the larger towns. This powder was conveyed in barrels, and these were stood on the ground near the gun during battle. Safety precautions were so bad that serious accidents were common during battles.

To these twenty-three guns which Cromwell took to Ireland were added the four demi-culverin which had been captured by Michael Jones at Dungan's Hill; later Ireton was to employ four mortars captured at Drogheda and Wexford to reduce Limerick. One of these fired a phenomenal ball of two hundredweights. All the shot employed in those days was, of course, solid; such

7

refinements as shrapnel were reserved for later and equally inhuman days.

There was a contemporary sneer that the officers of Cromwell's army were "factious and low-born sectaries . . . tradesmen, brewers, tailors, goldsmiths, shoemakers and the like". This may have been true, but so far as Cromwell was concerned the only qualification for a commission was competence; the only quality in which he was interested was leadership. Would the officer lead a charge? Would he set the proper example both in his public life as a soldier and in his private life as a puritanical saint? If the answer was yes, then he deserved well of the State and was fit to be her martial servant. The officers who went to Ireland were those who had made arms their profession; most knew no other; few wished otherwise. Promotion then, as now, but only rarely in the intervening three hundred years, was only by merit. The claims of seniority were not completely disregarded if only because long service in itself was a sign of merit.

In the early days of the Civil War the parliamentary leaders were wont to consult with their immediate subordinates prior to every encounter. Success sustained this practice, but Cromwell was too great a commander to wish to share his responsibilities, with the consequential risks and glories, with his senior officers. Yet he was too shrewd a judge of men not to realize that the appearance of consulting with the general was a marvellous sustenance to the authority of his regimental commanders. He reorganized the councils so that they became the convenient way in which he could issue his orders, while at the same time they would provide him with timely warnings of any administrative incompetence. The submission of his plans to his regimental commanders was to convince them of their rectitude, and to ensure that any deviation made necessary in the heat of battle would have the same ultimate objective; it was not for blind obedience but for intelligent co-operation that they were made privy to Cromwell's plans.

One of the great causes of Cromwell's success in Ireland was his ability to feed his army. The universal incapacity of general officers throughout Europe at this time in this respect had led to the prolongation of wars and consequential suffering because no victory could ever be made complete. At the conclusion of every battle troops invariably halted to reap the fruits of their valour. They could do this and be fed, or they could starve. The conversion of an enemy retreat into a rout was rare indeed. The famines in Germany during the Thirty Years War were due to the habit of all commanders of plundering the land they occupied on the instant, and of not drawing supplies from as large a support region as possible. To overcome these difficulties Cromwell had two solutions: at first he would depend upon supplies reaching him by sea from England; later he would live off the land of Ireland, but he would pay for every turnip. He knew only too well that his victories would be hollow and empty if his rear were peopled by an embittered and truculent crowd, dispossessed, starving, defeated, coerced and humiliated; such treatment might be meted out to those who deserved it on the morrow of total success, but not before. This was why he refused to move without a reserve of ready funds and explains his strict discipline.

The basis of the Ironside ration scale was biscuit (described as bread) and cheese. The soldier was expected to subsist on a pound of biscuit and half a pound of cheese per day. He could supplement this by what he could buy locally out of his pay. As might be expected this would vary enormously according to district, time of year, and the normal processes of supply and demand. In the early days in Ireland this was limited to fresh vegetables, due to the devastations of the troubles; later red meat found its way into the military market, as well as poultry and cereals.

But the most remarkable feature of the Expeditionary Force was its own peculiar brand of discipline. After the suppression of the spring mutinies the behaviour of the troops improved greatly, and their obedience was both cheerful and prompt. From then on offences of any kind were speedily detected and as rapidly punished. For the most serious, such as a deliberate refusal to obey orders, death was inflicted; for the less serious, whipping, humiliation and fines were imposed. Drunkards, oath-takers and similar malefactors were usually put in the stocks, the pillory or made to ride the wooden horse (sit astride some planks on edge with muskets tied to their feet). The true test of discipline is necessarily the determination of the private soldier to obey his orders; by this touchstone, the Ironsides formed the greatest fighting band of all time. Yet it is worthy of note that it was not the rigour with which the discipline was imposed, but the spirit with which it was accepted that really distinguishes this army. Personal piety was the fundamental passion of the rank and file; they would not tolerate among their comrades the expression of notions contrary to their morals and to their own puritanical Christianity. Antinomians, who said that moral laws were not binding on them, were dismissed from the service quite regularly. Cromwell complained of "profane persons, blasphemers, such as preach sedition, the contentious railers, evil-speakers who seek by evil words to corrupt good manners, persons of loose conversation, walking disorderly and not according but contrary to the Gospel . . . The discipline of the army is such that a man would not be suffered to remain there of whom we could take notice he was guilty of such practices as these."

When a minister's sermon contained unorthodox views or his behaviour was felt to be improper, these troops were not averse to telling him so, and that immediately. A Captain Pretty of Ireton's regiment ordered a minister out of the pulpit because he had been drunk the previous night and was not fit to preach. A Lieutenant Webb interrupted the sermon at Steeple Ashton by calling the minister "the black frog of Revelation"; his commanding officer sustained him by calling the minister Antichrist from the same pulpit the following Sunday. Competent ministers were hard to find, and consequently "the soldiers endeavoured the mutual edification of one another by exhortation on the Lord's Days". This freedom of preaching among all ranks produced every variety of belief and every variant of extravagance. Cromwell made no attempt to impose uniformity, and permitted every possible heterodoxy which did not involve the security of the State. This decision was to be reversed after the Restoration, and not repeated for two hundred years. The result in Ireland was twofold: under the constant pressure of a uniform religious opposition, Puritanism with all its glories and defects, but unsustained from across St George's Channel, was to wither and die in the south; but sustained and reinforced by refugees from another ecclesiastical persecution in Scotland, it was to inherit the north.

This then was the army which began to disembark on the banks of the river Liffey in the late summer of 1649. With it a new chapter in the history of Ireland was to open and the playing of

English guns on the walls of Irish garrison towns was to sound a knell for the forces of disorder. It heralded the commencement of the most important immigration Ireland has known, with a concomitant land settlement. Into the strife-torn land a substantial unifying element was being introduced. These men were masters and they intended that all should know it.

The preparation of the expedition is written up in Cromwell's own words, preserved by:
T. Carlyle: *Oliver Cromwell's Letters and Speeches* (London, 1849).
The Organization of the Expeditionary Force was the subject of the Ford lectures at Oxford 1900–1, and published under the title of:
C. H. Firth: *Cromwell's Army* (Methuen, 1902).

CHAPTER 5

The Storm of Drogheda

ON 15 AUGUST 1649 the *John* arrived in the estuary of the
Liffey. The people of Dublin, fearful of the advent of either Royal
or Catholic Government, welcomed Cromwell with open arms
and every manifestation of public joy. As the new Lord Lieutenant made his way from the quay towards the Castle in the open
carriage sent down for him by Michael Jones, the populace surged
around, shouting and cheering. Near College Green his coach was
brought to a standstill by the throng. Cromwell stood up, removed
his hat, and raised his hand to call for silence. After the din had
subsided he spoke. The actual text of his words has not survived,
if indeed a shorthand note was ever made, but from paraphrases
and reports we know the substance of what he said. After thank-
ing God for bringing him safely to Ireland and acknowledging the
loyalty of the Dublin people, he declared that Divine Providence
had required him to restore to them their just liberties and their
properties. He promised that all persons whose hearts' affections
were real for the carrying on of this great work against the barbarous and bloodthirsty Irish, their confederates and adherents,
for propagating Christ's Gospel and establishing Truth and Peace,
and for restoring this "bleeding Nation of Ireland to its former
happiness and tranquillity", should find favour and protection
from the Parliament of England and him; indeed they might
expect "such rewards and gratuities as might be answerable to
their merits". At the end of this impromptu oration the crowd
cheered themselves hoarse; Cromwell had completely won their
hearts; they knew instinctively that this man with the

reinforcements they had seen landing steadily over the last few weeks would put an end to the alarms and miseries of the previous eight years.

Oliver passed on into the Castle, to meet Michael Jones and hear from that officer how the affairs of the Commonwealth were prospering. We may appreciate what they said to each other by reconstructing the situation as it than existed.

The Commonwealth Army consisted of two very different elements. The Anglo–Irish of the Pale, the seedy adventurers of the past and the desperadoes of the Protestant Ascendancy, about 6,000 strong, were joined to the stern unbending Puritans, veterans of the English Civil War, disciplined by religious bigotry, the rigour of martial exercises, practical experience and the ardour of their officers, about 4,000 strong. The former, debauched and dissolute, were officered by barely competent men, and suffered from the eternal vices of drink and women. The latter were the advance party of the New Model, and it was to their standards that the former were to be brought in discipline, training and behaviour. This army was deployed in two parts: the bulk were in and around Dublin, the balance were besieged in Derry, 150 miles away. The latter were in a bad way, some of it of their own making, but they could be supplied by sea. The force in Dublin was in fine fettle, especially after their victory at Rathmines. The naval force in Irish waters was commanded by Sir George Ayscough, a zealous parliamentary officer who had suppressed a Royalist mutiny the previous year. Already he ensured that no substantial foreign aid reached Ormonde; he was now busy supervising the safe arrival of the Ironsides and their equipment.

Although Ormonde's army had been defeated at Rathmines his presence with a force still being increased by the steady arrival of reinforcements was a serious menace to Cromwell. This army stretched from the northern slopes of the Wicklow Hills in a great arc across the Liffey to somewhere near Swords. Within its ranks were to be found every party hostile to the parliament of England: old Irish, Anglo–Irish Catholics and Royalists, Scots from Ulster, Presbyterians from the Covenanting shires of Scotland, the disaffected and the desperadoes. Brave, determined men led by a devoted servant of the Crown, they lacked cohesion, pay and discipline. They all fought for the King; they also fought one another for the privilege of advising him. They distrusted one another's future intentions, and because they watched each other so closely, they did not watch the Ironsides closely enough! Their mutual hatreds were indeed quenched in the presence of Oliver's army, but their depredations had devastated the land they existed to protect, and from whose bounty they should have drawn an ample sustenance. Even so, victory, perhaps only a local success, might weld such a heterogeneous force into a formidable array. Success would replace the cloying effects of mutual distrust. At all costs and at any price Cromwell and Jones knew that they must meet and defeat Ormonde as soon as possible; any other action spelt disaster. There was no room to manoeuvre; there could be no retreat, for their backs were to the sea; they had to attack.

Oliver Cromwell quickly imposed discipline to his own high standards upon the Irish. He examined the records of all Anglo-Irish officers: those who were manifestly incompetent were "reduced", a polite euphemism for cashiered; the remainder together with the rank and file were solemnly warned to improve their behaviour. This purge was rapid, substantial and effective. On 21 August, Cromwell issued a proclamation which was posted on market-crosses, church doors, in ale-houses and anywhere else it could be both seen and read. Its distribution was ordered to cover all Ireland, but it only was seen within the English lines. It forbade all offences by the troops with particular reference to robbery, pillage and the infliction of cruelty; it promised the condign punishment of all offenders irrespective of rank; it offered to pay with ready money a fair price for all provisions brought into the lines; it promised that taxation would be fairly and rateably assessed and collected; and it imposed upon the English officers the duty of ensuring obedience. Such was the personal ability of Cromwell and such the zeal of his staff that the high standards desired were rapidly imposed upon the army, with benefit to all. It was soon apparent that Oliver's proclamations meant exactly what they said.

The problem of which way to turn out of Dublin for the first attack was fairly easy to solve. If Cromwell advanced westwards up the Liffey valley, he might cut Ormonde's army in two, but he would be plunging into the central bogs, unhealthy, difficult to cross, hopeless for his cavalry, away from the support of his ships and exposed to the sporadic attacks of bog-trotters and bandits. To turn north or south along the coast would avoid these difficulties. To go south would drive Ormonde back on his own communications; he would get steadily stronger as he retired, while Cromwell grew as steadily weaker as he detached troops to guard his communications. To strike north would take Ormonde away from his strength, would approach Derry with its beleaguered garrison, and would threaten the desultory recruitment of Covenanters from Ulster and Scotland. Behind the line of outposts to the north lay Drogheda. Commanding the road to Ulster and straddling the estuary of the river Boyne, it formed a pivot to the first natural defence line to contain a break-out from Dublin. Its importance had been properly evaluated by Ormonde, who sent there the best of his troops. If he could capture Drogheda Cromwell would consider himself reasonably safe; his land access to Ulster would be assured. If he then turned south his rear would be safe; and its loss would be a serious blow to the Irish. With the agreement of Jones and of his son-in-law, Henry Ireton, who had arrived shortly after him, Cromwell decided to attack Drogheda.

Ormonde probably guessed Oliver's intentions correctly; he lay with the main body of his army around Trim, hoping to be reinforced by a few thousand Ulster kerns under O'Neill. He was trying to reorganize his forces for a fresh assault on Dublin, but he needed plenty of time for this. However he had sent his most reliable subordinate, Sir Arthur Aston, with four regiments of English Royalists, two Irish regiments and a cavalry squadron of 200 horse to garrison Drogheda. The total force available for its defence came to about 3,000 men, of whom more than half were English.

For operations against Drogheda, Oliver decided to employ eight infantry regiments, six cavalry regiments, some troops of dragoons and eight field guns, totalling about 8,000 all ranks. This force was assembled at Collinstown on the evening of 30 August. The following day was devoted to the checking of their equipment, whilst the artillery was re-embarked on the ships in the Liffey. On 1 September they struck camp and marched off to establish themselves on Lord Barnwell's estate, three miles short of Drogheda; the following day, after driving in a few outposts, they occupied Ballygarth, in front of Drogheda. Oliver sited his artillery immediately, and his gunners set to work preparing the gun and mortar emplacements. Owing to contrary winds his ships failed to bring the field pieces forward as rapidly as he had hoped, and a week was to elapse before the Irish first heard his cannon. The guns were safely landed at the mouth of the Boyne on 5 September, and the next days were spent in dragging these cumbrous monsters along the tracks of the neighbourhood. The smaller pieces were soon in position, but it was not until Sunday, 9 September that the artillery was ready to begin the attack. During this period a few English soldiers had helped themselves to other people's property; three were shot on the Friday, and two more were hanged the next day. This was not only to deter others from going in search of plunder, but also to demonstrate to all, particularly the Irish peasantry, that Cromwell's justice was quite impartial.

Sir Arthur Aston was a brave, capable and experienced officer. He had served in the English Civil War with distinction, but by falling off his horse awkwardly he had broken his leg; the inefficiency of the medical services had led to the onset of gangrene, and the limb had to be amputated. He detested Cromwell, and longed to be the first Royalist to repulse the Ironsides from a fortified post. The defences of Drogheda had been improved by his skill and care. Outside the town to the south three parallel entrenchments had been dug, all overlooking the road to Duleek and Dublin; they were about one hundred and fifty yards long, and spanned the gap between St Mary's Church and the Duleek Gate. They were very different from the modern concept of trenches, and they had a different purpose; it was to compel an attacking enemy to delay his advance at the last instant before the final assault, thus enabling the defenders to repulse him. The excavated earth was thrown out behind the entrenchment, and behind this parados the defenders waited. Suitably designed these works would stop cavalry and were difficult for infantry. The walls of the old town lay in the rear of this position; they formed a position for a stand before street fighting began. Originally built in the Middle Ages, they were still in a moderate state of repair. Sir Arthur improved them further, but

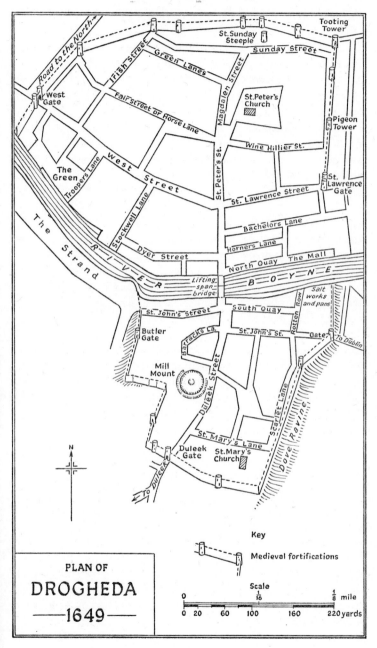

Tooting Tower

St. Sunday Steeple

Road to the North

Irish Street

Green Lanes

Sunday Street

West Gate

Fair Street or Horse Lane

Magdalen Street

St. Peter's Church

Pigeon Tower

Wine Hillier St.

The Green

Troopers Lane

WEST STREET

Stockwell Lane

St. Peter's St.

St. Lawrence Street

St. Lawrence Gate

Bachelors Lane

Horners Lane

The Strand

Dyer Street

North Quay

The Mall

R I V E R

Lifting span-bridge

B O Y N E

St. John's Street

South Quay

Salt works and pans

Rotten Row

Butler Gate

Barracks La.

St. John's St.

Gate

To Dublin

Mill Mount

Duleek Street

Scarlet Lane

Dove Ravine

St. Mary's Lane

Duleek Gate

St. Mary's Church

To Duleek

N

Key

Medieval fortifications

Scale

$\frac{1}{16}$ $\frac{1}{8}$ mile

0 20 60 100 160 220 yards

PLAN OF

DROGHEDA

—1649—

time was running out when his scouts brought him word that the English Army was advancing along the road from Dublin.

For the first week of contact the opposing forces contented themselves with the occasional skirmish along the outpost line. It is easy to be wise after the event, but this was Ormonde's opportunity. Cromwell's artillery was afloat, and his infantry were unprotected by this superior fire-power. An attack from the west, coupled with a sally from Drogheda would have postponed the evil day, and might have driven Cromwell back on Dublin. Even a raid on his communications at this stage would have compelled him to detach a portion of his sorely needed assaulting troops; at the crisis of the battle he had barely sufficient men to launch the final attack. But Ormonde lacked an efficient intelligence system; his staff was indifferent; and his forces were far too uncoordinated for synchronized attacks to be attempted. The opportunity was missed; it never recurred.

The old walled town and fortress of Drogheda was built on both banks of the river Boyne, about three miles from the sea, and as far as vessels could be expected to navigate in reasonable weather. Here quays were built for loading and unloading. Above this a bridge crossed the river. The town had been built on both banks, but the north side had been the more popular, and by this time only a quarter of the inhabitants lived on the south side. On the south there were two important features: a central earthwork surmounted by a masonry tower of great strength formed the nucleus around which the town had been built; and on the east side was a ravine, covered with briars and undergrowth and forming a convenient rubbish tip. At the confluence of the stream in this ravine, the Dove, with the Boyne were some salt pans where the poorest inhabitants tried to earn a living by extracting salt from the tidal reaches of the river.

The bridge across the Boyne was protected by a gatehouse and a drawbridge, so that the failure of the defence on one bank would not necessarily involve the rest of the town in disaster. A steep road led north from the bridge to the parish church of St Peter some two hundred and fifty yards away. Within the walls, which formed a circle of about three hundred and fifty yards radius, stood the rest of the town. Numerous gardens and orchards gave visual evidence of the security, wealth and amiable nature of the inhabitants. The walls were all strengthened by towers and gate-houses along their length. These were sited where roads left the town or where the direction of the wall changed. In two places they were weak—along the ravine above the Dove and, particularly adjacent to St Mary's Church where the angle was unprotected by any outwork.

When Cromwell and his officers examined Drogheda, they saw both its strength and its weakness. The dominating position of the Mill Mount and the importance of the single bridge impressed themselves on Cromwell's mind. He knew he must seize both at the same time, otherwise reinforcements could be channelled to either as necessary. He realized that the bridge itself was in-defensible, but it could be destroyed or the lifting span could be raised. If Sir Arthur chose to abandon the southern garrison a fresh assault, expensive in both casualties and time, would be necessary to reduce the northern part of the town. The main assault must carry his troops in great numbers through the breach to sweep round the Mill Mount and to seize the bridge intact.

On Sunday, 9 September Cromwell ordered his artillery to bombard St Mary's Church. The steeple of this church provided Sir Arthur with an important observation post, and on the tower from which the steeple sprang a number of mortars had been sited. Cromwell's guns had been sited about five hundreds yards away at the very limit of their useful range; but the trajectory of Aston's mortars, in spite of their elevation, was insufficient for the necessary counter-battery work. Under these conditions it was not long before the mortar position became untenable, and with it the value of the observation post. During the day an incessant hail of solid shot was rained upon the church, the churchyard and the wall which surrounded it. Although the casualties among the defenders were light, the effect upon the structures was substantial, and the English gunners were heartened by the sight of the damage they were causing.

The following morning, after a night of desultory skirmishes and some patrol activity, the English guns again opened fire on the southern defences of Drogheda, concentrating on the sector from the Duleek Gate to St Mary's Church and above the Dove stream. The garrison had spent the night trying to repair the damage of the previous day, but their efforts were soon dissipated by the accurate fire of the English guns. By midday great breaches had been torn in the walls and gaping holes riddled St Mary's steeple. Meanwhile the English cavalry had crossed the Boyne to the westward, and by vigorous patrolling were preventing any real access to or from the northern part of the town. Drogheda was now surrounded, and the southern walls had been breached. Accordingly Cromwell sent Sir Arthur a summons to surrender the town in accordance with the laws and customs of war; he added that Sir Arthur would know what to expect if the request were to be refused.

Sir Arthur had long realized that he would be beseiged, and that such a position would be one of the greatest danger. But he believed that he could hold out for a protracted period; that with the onset of autumn and the presence of a vigorous Irish Army in the neighbourhood, Cromwell would be compelled to raise the siege by November at the latest. The southern portion of the town was held by his own regiment, and commanded by his second-in-command, Sir Edmund Verney. The total force of 2,500 foot and 300 horse was believed to be in good heart; there was an ample sufficiency of supplies; the Protestant inhabitants had all been ejected because they might have represented a source of danger; and Sir Arthur knew that Cromwell's supply route could be cut by Irish raiders or made impassable by rain. Even if he lost South Drogheda, Sir Arthur felt that the northern part could hold out for a further period which might be indefinitely protracted. Cromwell would probably require most, if not all, his artillery on the north bank of the Boyne; moving it there would be a great time-waster. In the last post to Trim, just before the town was completely surrounded, Sir Arthur had promised Ormonde that he would see it out to the end. Cromwell's summons to surrender was ignored.

On Tuesday, 11 September, Cromwell's preparations were complete. Writing to Mr Speaker Lenthall, Cromwell described how his guns breached two sections of the wall adjacent to St Mary's Church. "About five o'clock on the evening, we began the Storm: after some hot dispute we entered, about seven or eight hundred men; the Enemy disputing it very stiffly with us. And indeed, through the advantages of the place, and the courage God was pleased to give the defenders, our men were forced to retreat quite out of the breach, not without some considerable loss; Colonel Castle being there shot in the head, whereof he presently died; and divers officers and soldiers doing their duty killed and wounded." Although the first attack had been repulsed, they had succeeded in carrying the southern entrenchments where the Ironsides had killed forty or fifty defenders. A fresh assault was then organized by Cromwell in person. This time after a very stiff resistance St Mary's Church was captured. Colonel Wall, who commanded the defence here, was killed, and this caused a sudden panic among his troops. They turned and ran for the bridge about two hundred yards away down the hill. They were pursued by the assaulting English. In their haste they omitted to raise the drawbridge; defenders and attackers crossed it together. Meanwhile a substantial party of Ironsides had surged up around the Mill Mount where Sir Arthur Aston had taken refuge with about 250 men. Cromwell's immediate objectives had now been reached, and the defenders were hopelessly separated.

In his letter home Cromwell went on to write about the battle at the Mill Mount, describing it as "a place very strong and of difficult access; being exceedingly high, having a good graft, and strongly palisaded. The Governor and divers considerable officers being there, our men getting up to them, were ordered by me to put them all to the sword. And indeed, being in the heat of action, I forbade them to spare any that were in arms in the town." The Ironsides burst into the Mill Mount, and began to cut down the garrison. It was widely believed that Sir Arthur's wooden leg was filled with gold coin; when he was found the limb was wrenched off; when it was found to be only wood the infuriated Ironside used it to batter the unfortunate commander to death. Sir Arthur's belt was found to contain 200 gold sovereigns, and these were promptly expropriated by the victorious troops.

Cromwell crossed the bridge to find that "about 100 of the enemy possessed St Peter's Church steeple, some the West Gate, and others a strong round tower next to the gate called St Sunday's. These being summond to yield to mercy, refused. Whereupon I ordered the steeple of St Peter's Church to be fired, when one of them was heard to say in the midst of the flames: 'God damn me, God confound me; I burn, I burn'." It is generally computed that about 1,000 were killed or burnt in and around St Peter's Church that night. Cromwell thought that 2,000 were killed in all Drogheda on that occasion. There can be no doubt that the parliamentary propaganda had so worked up the troops that they genuinely believed that the defenders of Drogheda had been personally responsible for the massacres of the Protestants eight years previously; they felt that the work they were doing was merely righteous execution on barbaric and treacherous savages. It was probably as well that they did not realize that at least half the garrison were English Catholics.

Desultory action went on through the night. In the morning the two remaining strong points were summoned to surrender; one did so. In the other about 130 refused to yield. Cromwell posted a guard round it to prevent any attempt at escape, knowing that thirst and hunger would soon compel them to capitulate. In spite of their predicament, the defenders sniped at the guard, killing some of them. Cromwell accordingly ordered his men to storm the tower. They did so, capturing the garrison. "When they submitted," Cromwell wrote, "their officers were knocked on the head; and every tenth man of the soldiers killed; and the rest shipped for the Barbadoes. The soldiers in the other Tower were all spared, as to their lives only; and shipped likewise for the Barbadoes."

Once all formal resistance was at an end, Cromwell permitted his troops to plunder the town indiscriminately. This was the usual reward for success in the seige of fortresses throughout Europe at the time. Believing that Catholic priests had provided the moral stiffening of the defence, and in some cases they had served as officers, the Ironsides sought out these men and killed them. One put to death was Father Peter Taafe, younger brother of Lord Taafe, one of Ormonde's field commanders. Sir Edmund Verney was found and shot on Saturday, 15 September; Colonel Boyle shared his fate the next day.

Numerous computations of the casualities have been made, both at the time and since. Hugh Peters, the famous Independent chaplain, reported in a letter of 15 September that "Tredagh is taken. 3,552 enemy and 64 English killed. None spared." The next day in a very short letter to Bradshaw, Cromwell doubted if more than thirty of the garrison had escaped, of which only one was an

Owen Roe O'Neill

Oliver Cromwell

officer; later he reported the number of slain as exceeding 2,800 enemy, some inhabitants and not 100 English. A printed official list prepared for parliament brought the casualties up to nearly 3,000 besides the inhabitants who had fought beside the troops and shared their fate. Richard Bellings, Secretary of the old Confederacy, thought the total slain amounted to about 4,000. And an eyewitness wrote to the Marquis of Newcastle that "there were butchered near 3,000 soldiers, and those reputed the best the Kingdom afforded". The numbers given by Hugh Peters are probably the best since as a chaplain he would have supervised the burial of the dead in the numerous grave-pits around the town; some may have been drowned, and others buried during the bombardment, so his figures may err on the small side, but the discrepancies are not likely to be very material. The killing of 3,500 in Drogheda was to have both immediate and long term effects.

Cromwell had little doubt that the slaughter was "a righteous judgement of God upon these barbarous wretches, who have imbrued their hands in so much innocent blood; and that it will tend to prevent the effusion of blood for the future. Which are the satisfactory grounds to such actions, which otherwise cannot but work remorse and regret." Ormonde himself reported: "It is not to be imagined how great the terror is that those successes and the power of the rebels have struck into this people. They are so stupefied, that it is with great difficulty that I can persuade them to act anything like men towards their own preservation." Sir Phelim O'Neill, in words which have rung through history, declared in despair: "If Cromwell had taken Drogheda by storm, if he should storm Hell, he will take it."

The flower of Ormonde's army had been destroyed, and the fury of the destruction was the principal feature of its disappearance. It struck an awesome knell in the hearts of the Irish: whose turn would it be next? The balance of power had tipped in Cromwell's favour at the battle of Rathmines; there was now no power in all Ireland to withstand the onset of his troops. Time would be the only factor in consummating the utter destruction of all forces hostile to the parliament of England. Three years were to pass before the last vestiges of Ormonde's authority had gone, but already this consequence was as sure as night following day.

8

The Proclamation by Cromwell of 24 August 1649 is to be found in Carlyle, as is his correspondence with Mr Speaker Lenthall. The Story of the Storm of Drogheda has been told by innumerable pens, none of which can ever be free from bias. The story as told in *The Nineteenth Century* of 1912 and 1913 is probably the one most free from the passions aroused by this celebrated occasion.

CHAPTER 6

The Campaign in the South

AFTER the storming of Drogheda, Cromwell considered his next move. Should he continue northwards, obliterate the resistance in Ulster and relieve Derry? Should he turn west to attack Ormonde near Trim? Or should he turn south to harry the Irish in Leinster and Munster? Suspecting that the Ulstermen were only lukewarm in their support for Ormonde, Cromwell ordered Colonel Venables with two infantry regiments and a squadron of cavalry to march northwards to raise the seige of Derry and beat down any resistance in Ulster. Venables captured the fortress of Dundalk intact on 13 September, and went on to occupy Carlingford, opening up another port, a few days later. His success here brought in a booty of forty barrels of powder, seven assorted cannon, 1,000 muskets and 500 pikes. He captured Newry on 18 September. Oliver's northern flank was secure.

Whilst Venables was marching off to deal with Ulster, Oliver learnt that Ormonde's main body at Trim was moving. He sent a cavalry regiment off to capture some prisoners and so confirm the news. They galloped through Trim and returned with the news that Ormonde was moving south and making for the bogs and mountains of central and southern Ireland. The menace to the Pale had been removed, and Oliver was free to turn in any direction he wished.

As a result of this, the main body of the English Army left Drogheda in the third week of September to march back to Dublin. With them went their guns, their baggage and their prisoners. It would be wrong to imagine that the prisoners formed

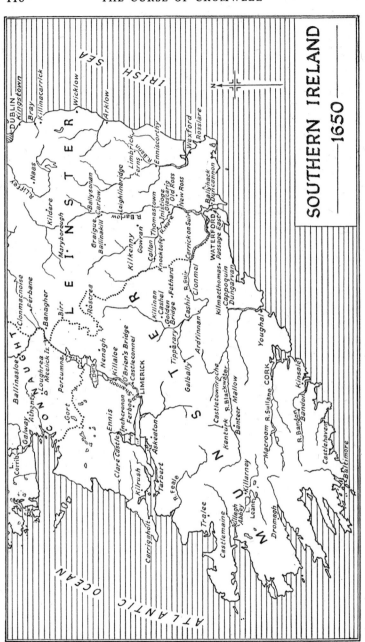

SOUTHERN IRELAND
1650

a long column of dejected men surrounded by guards; instead they were split up among the different regiments and employed by them on the hardest and most degrading tasks. They had to carry the heaviest loads, to assist in all river crossings, to extract waggons and guns from morasses on the road, to erect bivouacs for their new masters; and all this on the scantiest of rations, unshod, unclothed and unhoused. It was enough that they had not been shot. On arrival in Dublin they were lodged in the dungeons of the castle to await shipment to the West Indies.

After a short rest in Dublin, Cromwell's army marched southwards again on 23 September. There was little Irish opposition; only scouts watched their progress along the coast road through Bray and Wicklow. They arrived in Arklow on 27 September, where they halted for supplies to arrive by sea. The devastations of previous years showed clearly along the route from Killinacarrick, the first Irish fort fourteen miles from Dublin, all the way to Arklow. As before the heavier artillery pieces were left behind to follow down by sea. Oliver knew he could travel faster without such an encumbrance, and the benefits of sea-power meant that he need never be deprived of his guns or his baggage for long when he needed them.

On 29 September the Ironsides resumed their march, driving the Irish garrison out of Limbrick, capturing Ferns Castle and camping for the night in the environs of Enniscorthy. The castle there surrendered the next day, and its stock of arms, cannon and supplies fell into Cromwell's hands. A monastery was evacuated there; the friars ran away at the approach of the English. The town itself, left undamaged by the Irish, was not molested.

On 1 October the Ironsides crossed the river Slaney and prepared to invest the town of Wexford, which lies on the southwestern bank of the river where it debouches into Wexford Harbour. It was protected by its own medieval walls and a great earthwork fifteen feet across, about half a mile in circumference on the landward side; there was a castle at the south-eastern end of the wall, and only a narrow bridge gave access to the opposite shore of the harbour. Below the bridge a series of quays and staithes demonstrated the importance of the place to trade, and here were built small coasting vessels. The access from the north was still in the hands of the Irish, and Cromwell's communications were far too tenuous to supply his forces if operations round Wexford were protracted. A large and partly re-invigorated army lay perilously close to the road from Dublin; in fact a contingent moving to the relief of Wexford was to cross it in each direction during the siege. Cromwell's nearest port was Arklow, two days march away and unserviceable in bad weather; Rosslare did not then exist, and the other ports in the vicinity were firmly in Irish hands. The chill winds of autumn were beginning to blow, bringing with them rain to make life for the troops uncomfortable and to increase the incidence of sickness. Cromwell's safety depended on the rapid capture of Wexford.

Wexford was defended by Colonel David Sinnot and 3,000 men. Competently handled from within and sustained by an active and aggressive guerrilla without, Wexford should have been capable of withstanding a siege of some duration; but since Drogheda the fame of the Ironsides, their zeal and speed, had impaired the morale of the Irish. Sinnot's only alternative was to try and protract negotiations with Cromwell, thus putting off the evil day; but this line of approach did not commend itself to Cromwell. Neither he nor his men had any desire to spend the autumn in a leaking tent outside some truculent Irish town.

Cromwell wrote to Lenthall afterwards and described Sinnot's negotiations. Cromwell began by sending a demand for surrender on 3 October to prevent the effusion of blood and to preserve the town from ruin. Sinnot replied that he had no authority to surrender, but he would convene the town council to consider the matter and he would reply by noon the following day; in the meanwhile he asked for a cessation of arms. Cromwell agreed to expect the answer by noon, but he refused the cessation of arms "because our tents are not so good a covering as your houses, and for other reasons". This must have meant that he would continue his light artillery and musket fire, but would not launch his infantry to the attack. The next day Sinnot offered a conference and a treaty and suggested eight o'clock the next morning for their first meeting. This made Cromwell angry, but he asked Sinnot what his proposals were and he put a time limit of an hour on the answer. Sinnot protested at this ultimatum, rejected it, but again announced that he would send out his plenipotentiaries at eight o'clock the following morning.

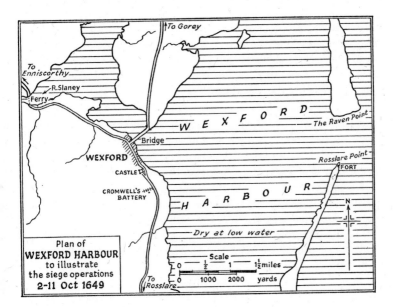

Plan of
WEXFORD HARBOUR
to illustrate
the siege operations
2-11 Oct 1649

Modern harbour draining and building works have modified the plan shown here. The chapel used as a prison for Protestants lay just to the North of the Castle, and hulk had been moored close to the Bridge.

To the east of Wexford lies a sandy spit of land protecting the harbour; at the root of this spit lay the village of Rosslare and at its tip a fort, garrisoned by the Irish and protected from the land by the narrowness of the spit and from the sea by the shoals of the harbour entrance. This position was further protected by a 12-gun frigate whose fire could rake any force sent along the sand spit. Michael Jones was ordered to clear the enemy out of this fort on 5 October. Accordingly he took a troop of dragoons and, covered by the early morning mist, they crossed the spit to capture the fort with ease, seizing as well the seven guns mounted there. With the lifting of the mist the dragoons turned the captured guns on the frigate; a passing ship of the English fleet joined the fight, and the frigate surrendered. A picket-boat with orders from Sinnot also fell into the hands of the English.

Cromwell could now use the entrance to Wexford harbour and bring into play that superiority conferred by sea-power; in particular he could land his heavy guns. But whilst Jones' troop was attacking the fort, the Earl of Castlehaven, commanding the advance guard of an Irish Army arrived on the opposite side of the harbour. He offered Sinnot a reinforcement of 500 men. Sinnot knew that to accept the relief would merely swell the Irish casualty list; yet to reject it would create despondency in his own lines. Accordingly he sent another message to Cromwell explaining that Castlehaven was his superior and would have to approve any proposals, but he would not "trifle out time". Cromwell cut him short on 6 October with a note revoking all previous negotiations, but "when you have cause to treat, you may send for another safe-conduct". Meanwhile Cromwell was landing his guns from the fleet and his men were dragging them into position.

On 7 October Ormonde arrived with the main body of the Irish on the opposite side of the harbour. His strength was over 3,000 men, and he, too, offered a substantial reinforcement. Sinnot declined this assistance. As it was both futile and dangerous to remain where he was, Ormonde marched away again. Jones was ordered to pursue them with 1,500 cavalry, but the Irish had disappeared into the swamps and thickets, so Jones returned disappointed.

On 11 October Cromwell ordered his artillery, which had now been mounted, to open fire on the castle. Sinnot realized that he

could no longer resist; he asked for safe-conducts for his representatives. Cromwell granted these and suspended his bombardment.
The plenipotentiaries included the commander of the castle
garrison, and they came out with proposals which Cromwell
thought impudent; but he replied that if the garrison laid down
their arms, the rank and file could go home, the officers would be
made prisoner and the town would not be pillaged, but he required
the answer within the hour. The castle commander knew that
further resistance was pointless and resolved to make his own
terms. He surrendered his charge, and the Ironsides occupied the
castle. The castle dominated the town, and the Irish quit
the adjacent walls. The hour was up, and the Ironsides entered
the town. The Irish made a stand in the market-place, but the
impetuosity of the English attack was too much for them. A
furious fight followed, and two atrocities came to light: about 150
Protestants had been interned in a hulk in the harbour; this had
been sunk and the prisoners drowned; another batch of Protestants
had been immured in an old chapel and left there without food
or water to die of thirst or starvation. Once these facts were known
to the Ironsides no further quarter was given and over 2,000 Irish
were killed. A few managed to escape across the bridge, and they
melted into the countryside; once they could no longer interfere
with his plans, Cromwell had no further interest in them.

The Ironsides now plundered Wexford systematically. The
larger items of loot, however, were reserved for the State. Writing
home Cromwell itemized the haul: "great quantities of iron, hides,
tallow, salt, pipe- and barrel-staves, nearly 100 guns, three ships
(one of 34 guns and another of 20 guns), a frigate of 20 guns still
on the stocks and other smaller vessels." Cromwell now felt safe
again; he had acquired another advance base with a great and
sheltered harbour, and from here he could prosecute his plans to
conquer the south.

Leaving Colonel Cooke with a small garrison in Wexford,
Cromwell left the town on 16 October. He arrived at New Ross,
twenty-four miles away, the next day. It was defended by Lucas
Taafe, another brother of Lord Taafe, and 1,000 infantry. The
town stands on the east bank of the river Barrow, shortly below
its confluence with the river Nore and fifteen miles from the sea
into which these waters debouch through Waterford Harbour.

On the west side of the river lay Ormonde with the main body of the Irish Army. Again he was faced with the problem: should he abandon the place and suffer the inevitable decline in morale? or should he defend it and lose both the town and its garrison? Ormonde left the decision to Taafe. As usual Cromwell began by demanding the surrender of the town. Taafe did not reply; so Cromwell ordered his men to prepare positions for his guns which were following along from Wexford.

At dawn on 19 October the English batteries opened fire. This heralded the end and Taafe knew it. He offered to surrender the town on terms and asked for a cessation while negotiations took place. Refusing the cessation, Cromwell, however, offered to allow the Irish troops to march away and protect the inhabitants from violence if the town were surrendered. By now the walls had been breached and the storming parties were forming up. To save his own and his soldiers' lives, Taafe had to capitulate immediately; he did so, and inquired if liberty of conscience would be granted to those who remained. "I meddle not," replied Cromwell, "with any man's conscience. But if . . . you mean a liberty to exercise the Mass, . . . that will not be allowed of." Taafe was allowed to cross the river to rejoin Ormonde who then retreated up the valley of the Nore to Kilkenny. The continuing refusal of battle by Ormonde was demoralizing, and its first sign was the refusal of the English element of the garrison of New Ross to march out with Taafe; they stayed to join the Ironsides.

The occupation of this pleasant town provided the Ironsides with some very welcome shelter in this rainy autumn, while the capture of Taafe's artillery augmented the already substantial fire power of the invaders. It was now, too, that Oliver's stern discipline began to reap its reward: supplies were brought into the English lines in ample profusion by the local people, who were sure of immediate payment in coin for all they sold. Money was a commodity they had not seen for a long time! Even the most zealous Royalists were forced to admit that the Parliamentary Army was much better fed than the Irish. It was due to their superior supply system that the English managed to maintain their health, in spite of their encampments being in unhealthy places and unhygenic conditions. Cromwell's other remedy was to keep on the move; and he managed to do this until December.

The next stage in the reduction of Ireland was to occupy the major ports along the south coast, and from these to drive north in parallel columns to conquer all Munster and drive Ormonde into the barren wastes of the west, where he would be compelled to split up his forces. A very secret correspondence had been opened with a number of English residents in Cork and Youghal; these were merchants whose trade had stagnated since the troubles started, but whose former prosperity excited the envy of the Irish. They indicated that they would do everything in their power to persuade their fellow countrymen to return to their allegiance to England, but they wanted to know that seaborne assistance or a landward diversion would prevent any Irish reprisal. With this Cromwell was pleased, and in due course he gave the desired encouragement.

The next port Cromwell wished to take was Waterford; but it lay on the opposite bank of the river Suir and was difficult to approach. Ormonde's army was still intact in Kilkenny and could menace his communications through New Ross with Wexford; and the forts at the entrance to the harbour would hamper the landing of supplies. To begin his campaign, Michael Jones was sent with about half the Ironside effectives to reduce Duncannon, a small post on the east of the harbour and about three miles from Hook Head. Duncannon was defended by a Colonel Roche, but his men began to desert in great numbers. Ormonde promptly replaced the uninspiring Roche by Colonel Wogan, a deserter from the New Model who well understood the consequences of failure, and a party of his life-guard. This stiffening had the required results, and Jones had to subject Duncannon to a blockade. The weather turned against the English, and for a fortnight they lay in leaking, unhealthy bivouacs, hungry, wet and miserable. Wogan's constancy generated trust between the English and Irish, Catholic and Protestant elements of his force. By the beginning of November Jones had had enough; he struck camp and returned to New Ross.

By now Ormonde's hold on the Munster ports was disintegrating. On 16 October Cork had risen: the English element of the garrison, supported and encouraged by the merchants, expelled the governor and ejected the Irish troops. Within a week Inchiquin's English had mutinied and marched off to join Cromwell.

As soon as he heard of the Cork rising Cromwell sent Lord Broghill, Colonel Phayr, who had conducted much of the secret correspondence, and Blake to the city. They arrived by sea on 3 November to be welcomed by a wildly enthusiastic crowd. With this the hold of Ormonde on his own troops was further weakened; the different parties sought to blame each other in their search for scapegoats. It was far easier to raise the age-old cry "We are betrayed", than to search for the real cause of the distress, and thus rectify the situation.

Meanwhile in Dublin the Commonwealth base was filled with troops, both reinforcements from England and the sick who had been discharged from hospital. At the end of October it was decided that they should be sent forward to join the main body of the army around Waterford. The confidence and ability of these men, coupled with the known incapacity of the Irish leadership, prompted the local command to send them forward by road rather than assemble shipping to send them round by sea. Thus a detachment of about 1,200 men, some hardened veterans, but most young recruits, a few on horseback but many on foot, with four cannon, commenced the militarily hazardous journey across hostile country in the face of superior numbers. Prudence kept them close to the sea as they marched southwards; sporadic resistance reminded them that Ireland was not yet conquered, and provided the recruits with a foretaste of battle. Just south of Arklow, Inchiquin with about 3,000 Irish decided to attempt their destruction. Here, where the road runs along the sea shore at the foot of the Wicklow Hills, was the natural defensive position: this was the ideal place to hem in the Ironsides and cut them up before help could reach them. It would be the scene for a massacre of Cromwell's famed Ironsides, a startling reverse to their invincible career. The Irish position was chosen with care, and all that the skill of capable sappers could do improved the site. A road block, protected by about 1,000 Irish, was set up at the southern end of the defile. An ambush of another thousand Irish was prepared for the northern end, whilst the remainder lined the high ground above the road. This was the Irish nut-cracker which, it was hoped, would put an end to their series of appalling defeats and a stop to the unbroken tide of Ironside success. Down the road in the late afternoon of 1 November came the Cromwellian phalanx;

marching with speed and vigour they hoped to reach Wexford before dark. Their advance guard descried the Irish position as the main body entered the defile. The English deployed on to the beach and continued their advance: the Irish attack then began and a fierce battle ensued on the sea shore. The tide was out and the full weight of an Ironside attack was developed on the southern exit. With this the Irish ambush broke cover at the northern entrance, and assaulted the English rear. The cannon were escorted by the rearguard, and were immediately brought into action to drive off the Irish. They did just this with terrible effect, and before long the beach was a scene of dreadful carnage. Discipline and training soon made their effects felt, and the battle degenerated into yet another Irish rout. As darkness closed in the last shots were fired from the cannon and the Ironsides resumed their march to obtain a night's shelter in Wexford well before midnight. Heartened by their success the little English force continued their march the next morning. Compelled to submit to superior ability the sullen and resentful Irish could only watch the triumphal progress from the surrounding hills. There was no further incident on this march, and Cromwell was glad to welcome this reinforcement in his camp outside Waterford.

Whilst Cromwell was establishing his military superiority in the south, Colonel Venables was crushing the Irish in Ulster. After the capture of Newry, he had scoured South Down and Armagh; but he overreached his communications near Portadown and was lucky to escape from the trap O'Neill had prepared for him. By the end of October Venables had successfully occupied Armagh, Lisburn and Belfast: he had yet to overcome the Royal fortresses in Charlemont and Carrickfergus, but he was in touch with patrols from Derry. In September he had sent Colonel Huncks' regiment by sea to reinforce Sir Charles Coote, who had not been slow to give them exercise. In October they had recaptured Coleraine and driven O'Neill out of Antrim and North Down. This meant that the only Irish officer capable of facing Cromwell was pinned down by the successful operations in the north as well as by his own sickness.

In September O'Neill had sent his nephew, Daniel, to tell Ormonde what he was doing. O'Neill was then at Omagh, in central Tyrone, planning to march to Westmeath. Whilst on his way there, his emissaries and Ormonde's met at Finea to agree that O'Neill should be Ormonde's commander in Ulster with a force of 6,000 infantry and 1,000 cavalry. In accordance with this agreement, too, he sent General O'Ferrall to the south with a brigade of 3,000 troops. He was preparing to follow when his health gave way, and he died on 6 November at Cloughoughter in County Cavan. This was a terrible blow to Ormonde, for O'Neill by his personality and competence had the ability to inspire ill-fed, ill-clad, unpaid troops to resist, even with some success, the finest professional soldiers in the world.

At this time Cromwell began a fresh attempt to obtain Waterford. He began by routing Inchiquin at Glascarrig just north of New Ross; Colonel Abbot, one of Ireton's commanders, captured Innistioge, eight miles up the river Nore; Colonels Reynolds and Ponsonby occupied Carrick-on-Suir, where a bridge gave easy access to the city of Waterford (it was also a country residence of Ormonde, and the provisions he had accumulated there for his family fell into Cromwell's hands). Althouth sickness, bad weather and the need to protect his communications reduced Cromwell's effective fighting strength to less than 7,000, he set out in mid-November from New Ross to cross the Suir at Carrick and arrived in front of Waterford three days later. Ormonde missed another opportunity to attack Cromwell and to drive him into the peninsula formed by the rivers Suir and Nore, where he would have been cut off from his land communications and some distance from the sea.

Cromwell sent the usual demand to Waterford for its surrender, but he received No for an answer. He settled down to besiege the town, but he could not stop access to the north by the Suir bridge; it was by this route that Ormonde offered them reinforcements. Remembering the trouble at Duncannon, the Waterford men announced that they would only trust Ulstermen, and so O'Ferrall with 1,500 men were sent to provide the material and moral stiffening the town required.

Seven miles away to the south-east of Waterford, on the western shores of the harbour, nearly opposite Duncannon, was the complementary fortress of Passage East. Beneath its guns was deep water where 300-ton ships could anchor and unload their cargoes in safety, but past which no enemy could go without grave danger.

Cromwell sent Jones to try and capture this place with a party of cavalry. The Ironsides soon surrounded the fort and opened fire with their light guns. The garrison was not commanded by Wogan, nor were they of the same stamp as those of Waterford; they asked if quarter would be given. Jones promptly agreed, and he occupied this important post without loss; with it came a gun position with two field pieces two miles further down the harbour.

During these operations the weather had been mild and dry; now it broke, and there was heavy rain with sleet and hail. The very low strength of his force, and the prospect of serious losses by sickness, prompted Cromwell to raise the siege on 2 December and move off to the ports of Dungarvan, Youghal and Cork, where his men might rest, and be supplied by sea. He was met the next day by Lord Broghill at Kilmacthomas with the great news that southern Munster was declaring for the English Parliament. The garrison at Dungarvan had revolted that morning; Bandon and Kinsale had followed the lead of Cork; while Castlehaven and Baltimore were expected to adhere in a few days. In spite of the appalling weather and their own exhaustion, the Ironsides marched into Dungarvan in high spirits. But Michael Jones died there on 10 December as a result of hardships during the campaign. "What England lost thereby," Cromwell wrote, "is above me to speak. I am sure I lost a noble friend."

As he left Waterford Cromwell had seen O'Ferrall's men entering the city on the opposite bank of the Suir. The two hostile armies were too far apart for a clash, but Cromwell must have smiled grimly, for his cavalry had swept the local countryside bare. Although the blockade had been lifted, the provisioning of Waterford would stretch Ormonde's facilities to the limit. Furthermore the immobilization of the best Irish field troops in that fortress, now seriously weakened by the loss of Passage East, gave Cromwell additional satisfaction.

Emboldened by the apparent removal of the Ironside threat, the people of Waterford urged O'Ferrall to attempt the recapture of Passage East. But there were no secrets in the Irish lines and Cromwell soon learnt of the scheme. Cromwell was now resting in Youghal, but his rearguard was still on the north bank of the river Blackwater near Cappoquin, about forty miles from Passage

East. Colonel Zanchy with about 300 cavalry was ordered to assist the garrison at Passage East; he left Cappoquin immediately. His progress was in Cromwellian style; he left the peasantry alone, but he killed every Irish soldier he could catch. Zanchy soon drove in O'Ferrall's picquets, and then encircled the Irish, who numbered about 500 infantry under Henry O'Neill, son of Owen Roe, and some artillery under Colonel Wogan. About 100 Irish were killed and the rest were captured, including O'Neill, Wogan and the commander of the post at Ballyhack. Writing to Lenthall, Cromwell told of the success and added about the prisoners: "Concerning some of these I hope I shall not trouble your justice."

Whilst O'Ferrall was attacking Passage East, Ormonde thought to assist by attacking Carrick-on-Suir; but co-ordination of effort was not his strong point, and it was a week after O'Ferrall's attack had failed that Ormonde moved off towards Carrick. The prompt payment of peasants for supplies also provided the Ironsides with early warning of what was afoot. Active patrolling by them soon disclosed the Irish movements, and by the time they reached the environs of Carrick they were thoroughly disheartened. The result of this foray was a foregone conclusion, and the Irish were soon streaming back to Kilkenny in rout, pursued by a relentless foe.

In Ulster, Carrickfergus, the last Royalist stronghold, surrendered in December, and the whole coastline was firmly in parliamentary hands. From their new bases the English vicegerents began to harry the Irish as never before. The dispossessed settlers of 1641 saw their own interests clearly, and they joined in the fray behind Colonel Venables. Their religious views were Puritan; their material interests were the improvement of trade; their enthusiasms were anti-Catholic; and their hopes were anti-Irish. Secure in the knowledge that overwhelming force was ultimately available to sustain them, they burst forth to exact a terrible retribution from those who had occupied their lands; for them only blood could cleanse the land; only by extermination of the Irish could they purchase safety.

In the Pale, life was starting to become placid once more. For the traders business was good. Cromwell's treasure chest was still fairly full, and now local taxation was beginning to replenish it. With the prompt payment for all military supplies, confidence

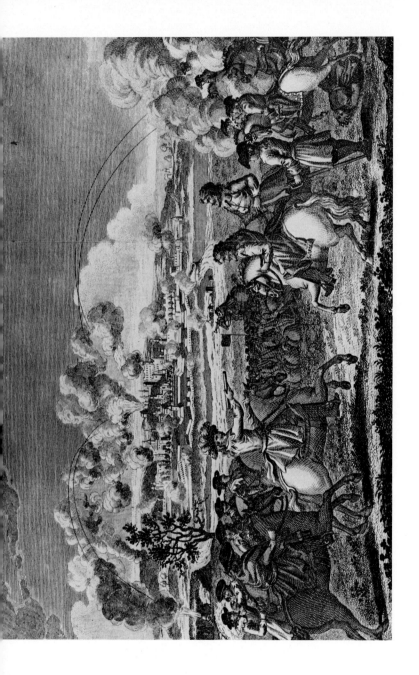

Oliver Cromwell taking Drogheda by storm

King Charles II

had returned, and with it prosperity; expansion and plans for the future had again become concepts in men's minds.

From Dungarvan Cromwell had moved to Youghal, and then after a short stay on to Cork, where he remained until the New Year of 1650. He only left the city to inspect his garrisons at Kinsale, Bandon and Mallow. In the wet and unpleasant weather he rested his troops in the various ports along the coast; they were quartered in the houses of the dispossessed Irish. Here they slowly recovered their health and spirits; the rheums and agues (colds and malaria) of the autumn disappeared, and in the early spring they were ready and fit to complete their task of conquering Ireland.

But across the lines in the rest of Ireland, life was grim, and the prospects bleaker. The perpetual shortage of food heralded the approach of famine. Now was added the additional curse of pestilence. The medieval blight of bubonic plague, spread by rats and nurtured by the absence of hygiene, was sweeping through the larger towns held by Ormonde. Its devastations were said to have been worse than those of the sword; and where overcrowding was common we need not doubt that the blow was as cruel as any the Ironsides could inflict.

In the general afflictions, medical, moral and material, which had struck Ireland, the priesthood was soon heard thundering denunciations and hurling anathema at the causes, real and imaginary. As in every other human crisis the opportunity was not to be missed to proclaim the consequences of sin, to urge upon the faithful the necessity of strict adhesion to their doctrines, and to remind men that the remission of their errors was dependent on their observance of the sacred laws including the payment of the proper tithes for the temporal maintenance of Mother Church. But for all this the Catholic Church remained the one enduring reality, the one unifying entity in the Irish camp. Only the decrees of the episcopate had any chance of universal obedience, only the moderating influence of the hierarchy could smooth the ruffled feelings of the turbulent. The prelates were both priests and Irishmen; eager to accept the responsibilities thus thrust upon them, they met at Clonmacnoise at the beginning of December 1649 to discuss the best way to discharge their duties. The place was well chosen: a monastery in the centre of Ireland at an inhospitable

9

spot on the banks of the Shannon, it was at once remote from the clash of arms yet by its central position it could ensure the rapid dissemination of any decision reached there.

These ecclesiastics saw the situation with clear and critical eyes; they realized that Cromwell's policy of paying immediately for supplies at proper prices was practised to eliminate unrest in his communications. They issued their first manifesto almost immediately: it was a general warning. They declared that Cromwell would stop at nothing to extirpate the Cathoic religion: for those who escaped execution or exile there would be enthralment. They pointed out that before the Civil War the English Parliament had decreed the expropriation of the estates of the Irish, that these enactments had been reinforced by the Ordinances of the Long Parliament and the decrees of the Council of State, and that when the resistance of the Irish had been beaten down, the policies in question would be executed with religious and pecuniary zeal. They reminded their readers of Cromwell's reply to Taafe's question at New Ross, that he would not allow the exercise of the Mass. At the conclusion of the war the adventurers who had put up the money for the re-conquest would call upon the troops to instal them in their estates, and what might these landlords be like?

A week later a second manifesto was issued. It laid bare the source of their troubles, and explained how the internecine rivalries of the different factions were to be ended. It declared that the feud between Rinnuccini's partisans and Ormonde's was pointless and was to be ended; in future they would be united for the Church, "the advancement of His Majesty's rights and the good of this nation in general". These manifestoes were followed by the necessary orders to put the policies into effect; they depended for their execution on the sanctions, not inconsiderable even then, of the Catholic Church. As Ormonde's power and influence declined, so the effects of Catholic pertinacity raised the prestige of the Church and her priesthood to even higher pedestals in the minds of the Irish.

In spite of communication difficulties these manifestoes and decrees spread through all Ireland. In the middle of January 1650 a copy reached Cromwell, who had re-established himself in Youghal. He replied immediately. He wrote: "for the Undeceiving of Deluded and Seduced People; which may be satisfactory to all that wilfully do not shut their eyes against the light." He pointed out that the clergy had appropriated the consent of the Irish laity who had not been represented at Clonmacnoise; that the distinction between clergy and laity existed only to enable the former to batten on the latter "for filthy lucre's sake", and to pretend to a superior sanctity so that they might "bridle, saddle and ride" the latter. He complained the he was described as "the common enemy." He reminded the Irish of the union of England and Ireland: "Englishmen had good inheritances . . . purchased with their money . . . from you and your ancestors. They had good leases from Irishmen for long times to come. They lived peaceably and honestly among you. You had . . . equal justice from the laws . . . You broke this Union! You, unprovoked, put the English to the most unheard of and most barbarous massacre (without respect of sex or age) that ever the Sun beheld. And at a time when Ireland was in perfect Peace. Is God, will God be with you?"

He proclaimed his faith in his own answer: "I am confident He will not!" He went on to criticize their claim to fight for the King; in reality they fought "in protection of men of so much prodigious guiltiness of blood". He went on: "You are a part of Antichrist, whose Kingdom . . . should be laid in blood. You have shed great store of that already; and ere long you . . . must have blood to drink; even the dregs of the cup of fury and the wrath of God which will be poured out unto you."

Then he spelt out the future that Ireland could expect. "I shall not, where I have power, and the Lord is pleased to bless me, suffer the exercise of the Mass . . . nor suffer you that are Papists, where I can find you seducing the People or by any overt act violating the Laws established; but if you come into my hands, I shall cause to be inflicted the punishments appointed." But if Catholics "walk honestly and peaceably" they would not suffer. It was a downright lie to suggest that he had come to "massacre, destroy and banish" them: "Give us an instance of one man since my coming into Ireland not in arms massacred, destroyed or banished, concerning . . . whom Justice hath not been done, or endeavoured." But on the other hand, "If the People run to arms by the instigation of their clergy or otherwise, such as God . . . shall give into my hands may expect that or worse measure from me, but not otherwise." He justified the forfeiture of rebel lands, but if the owners would submit he would examine their behaviour and mitigate the severities of the forfeiture if possible.

The message was clear, and the remedy simple. No one could complain that he did not know exactly where he stood. The option might be hard, but it was not impossible; to the exhausted rank and file of Ormonde's army it even contained the promise of a fair chance.

During that winter the Irish had a small success. A garrison had been left in Enniscorthy, where they occupied the castle. Noticing that the Ironside discipline was somewhat slack and their vigilance lax, some local Irishmen decided to try their hand at local surprise. They began by offering hospitality; then they gave the soldiers a feast; after the guests had departed the local girls came forward with whiskey. The soldiers forgot their cares, drank freely and too much: in their inebriated condition they could not resist the surprise attack, and Enniscorthy reverted to the control of the Irish. All the English were killed. As a result of this Cromwell ordered his garrisons to dispense with Irish servants; they must not be allowed inside English fortresses.

On 29 January 1650 Cromwell left Youghal at the start of his spring campaign. He despatched Colonel Reynolds with fifteen troops of cavalry and 1,000 infantry to march on Kilkenny by the shortest route across the Suir at Carrick; Major-General Ireton followed with the reserves, the artillery and the baggage. Cromwell himself with another fifteen troops of cavalry and about 250 infantry made a wide sweep to the west crossing the river Blackwater at Mallow, forty-five miles away, before turning towards Kilkenny. Throughout this march to Mallow and afterwards Cromwell was too far away from Reynolds and Ireton for mutual support. They overcame the risks by the speed of their movements. On 31 January Cromwell crossed the river Blackwater and seized a castle called Kilkenny near Mallow, where he left a garrison of thirty infantry. He met Broghill there and instructed him to occupy the region, to subdue any Irish troublemakers, and to watch Inchiquin in Limerick and Kerry. Broghill's vigour reduced Castletownroche nine miles away two days later. Cromwell seized Roghill Castle at the same time; and then crossing the Suir near Cahir "with very much difficulty", he advanced to Fethard. The weather so far had been mild, but then it deteriorated with wind and rain. Cold, wet and hungry the Ironsides searched for suitable bivouacs, while Cromwell sent his usual summons to the town: the governor of Fethard sent out two negotiators, and Cromwell bluffed them into surrender by the offer of liberal terms which he "was the willinger to give because [he] had little above 200 foot and neither ladders nor guns nor anything else to force them". At the same time the garrison in Cashel quit the place because of the presence of the Ironsides!

After a short rest Cromwell learnt that Reynolds had seized Callan, so he marched his troops across the twenty-five-mile gap to concentrate his whole force in close proximity to Kilkenny. Just before this Reynolds had surprised some of Ormonde's cavalry and taken prisoner two officers and some men. One of the officers had been responsible for the Enniscorthy affair and was hanged. There were three Irish-held castles in Callan; one surrendered and the Irish were allowed to depart; the other two refused to surrender, and were stormed; the garrisons were slaughtered. As Ormonde did not wish to give battle and Cromwell's siege artillery was scattered, Lord Colvil was left in Callan with a small force to watch Kilkenny, while Reynolds cleared the Irish out of Knocktofer, five miles away on the road to New Ross. Cromwell himself returned to Fethard and Cashel with the main body.

Broghill had thrust north meanwhile into County Limerick where he attacked a castle held by Sir Edward Fitzharris; when the surrender demand was refused, Broghill bombarded it until Fitzharris changed his mind. In accordance with the usual rules the rank and file were granted "quarter for life", but the officers were shot. Ireton had obtained possession of the bridge at Ardfinnan which enabled Cromwell to shorten his communications with the Munster ports. Thus after a fortnight's campaigning Cromwell had cleared much of southern Munster; he had shown again his military skill and the speed with which his troops could move; he had loosened Ormonde's hold on the Irish; and all this at a very low cost in English life, but now his treasure chest was becoming depleted.

Cromwell had required County Tipperary to pay £1,500 per month to help pay for the maintenance of the English troops there; other portions of subjugated territory were rateably assessed for

the same purpose; but these assessments hardly covered the cost of
the garrisons when they were static. Cromwell wrote to Mr
Speaker Lenthall urging that "if the marching army be not con-
stantly paid, . . . indeed it will not be for the thrift of England as
far as England is concerned for the speedy reduction of Ireland.
If the active force be not maintained, and all contingencies de-
frayed, how can you expect but to have a lingering business of it?"

Whilst Broghill covered Inchiquin in Limerick and Reynolds
watched Ormonde in Kilkenny, Cromwell himself eliminated the
Irish menace in Cahir "without the loss of one man", and captured
the bridges across the Suir at Killinan and Golden Bridge on the
Cashel to Tipperary road. Dundrum Castle was taken, and a post
established at Ballinakill, some twenty miles north of Kilkenny.
During the course of these skirmishes some senior officers of
Ormonde's horse were captured; three of these were found to
have served the Parliament in England but had since changed
sides: for such Cromwell had no mercy and they were shot. By
the beginning of March Cromwell was ready to blockade Waterford again, and to attempt the capture of Kilkenny.

At the same time Colonel Hewson left Dublin with a further
batch of reinforcements for Cromwell. As a result of the successful
action at Arklow in November, Hewson decided to march across
country instead of following the coast road, and thus save two
days. He discounted the military hazard of crossing hostile country
in close proximity to large enemy forces because of the speed with
which he could move, the superior discipline and excellent training
of his men. By the middle of March Hewson reached Ballysonan,
just north-east of Carlow. Lord Castlehaven and O'Ferrall covered
Kilkenny with their forces which were quartered around Carlow
and Leighlinbridge. To break up this Irish force, Cromwell
ordered Colonel Shilbourn with some cavalry from Wexford to
join Hewson, cross the river Barrow and march towards Carlow
as fast as they could. To divert his attention, Cromwell also sent
750 horse and 500 foot to attack Castlehaven's rear. This party
swept through north Kilkenny with little trouble, but when they
reached Graigue, near Carlow, there was no news of Hewson.
Accordingly they turned southwards along the west bank of the
river Barrow for some miles until they were in striking distance of
Castlehaven. As they were comparatively weak, and there was still

no news of Hewson, they turned south-westwards to Thomastown, a small walled town on the river Nore. The garrison there retired into a castle. Cromwell and Ireton, his son-in-law and now the President of Munster, then arrived with some guns. After these had opened fire, the Irish garrison surrendered; they were permitted to depart on promising never to bear arms against the Parliament of England again. Hewson had only just missed the party sent to meet him, but he stormed Leighlinbridge, and then advanced to join Cromwell at Gowran, then described as a populous town but now a typical sleepy village. Gowran was defended by a Colonel Hammond, a Kentish man who had been concerned in the second English Civil War; he refused to surrender, so Cromwell bombarded the place until he did. The rank and file and one officer, "a very earnest instrument to have the Castle delivered," were granted their lives; but all the other officers were shot and a Catholic priest hanged.

Ireton then returned to Fethard to send infantry forward to Cromwell and to take the artillery back to Waterford. He systematically reduced the outposts round the city, and by the end of March the Granny and Donkill had fallen. At the same time quarrels between the townspeople and O'Ferrall had provoked the Ulsterman and his troops to declare that they would serve no more in the south. They left by the last remaining route before Ireton closed it and returned to Ulster. The doom of Waterford, although delayed for five more months, was now certain, and Ireton sent his heavy guns back to Cromwell.

On 22 March Cromwell arrived at the outskirts of Kilkenny, which had two governors, one for the city and the other for the castle, a mayor and other civic functionaries, and an abundance of priests. Cromwell addressed himself to the "Governor, Mayor and Aldermen"; he came, "to endeavour the reduction of the City . . . to their obedience . . . to England; from which by an unheard-of Massacre of the innocent English, you have endeavoured to rend yourselves. You may have Terms such as may save you in your lives, liberties and estates according to what may be fitting for me to grant and you to receive. If you choose for the worst, blame yourselves."

The next day Sir William Butler, the city governor, replied that he intended to hold the town for the King; two days later he again refused to surrender. Cromwell now ordered the town to be shelled. A sizeable breach was forced, and on 26 March Colonel Ewer with 1,000 infantry was ordered to occupy the "Irish town", which he did for a loss of four men; meanwhile the main body of Cromwell's infantry attempted to storm the breach, but they were repulsed. When the storming party reached the breach they found that interior fortifications covered it. Colonel Ewer's men managed to carry some further works adjacent to the "Irish town" on the same side of the river. On 27 March a further attempt to carry the breach failed, but the Cromwellian bombardment continued and the Irish realized that soon it would be only too effective. On 28 March they asked for terms: the city and garrison were surrendered, the town was mulcted £2,000, and two principal citizens were taken hostage for its payment, and the troops were permitted to march out with "all the honours of War", but to disperse peacefully after marching for two miles. Writing to Lenthall, Cromwell expressed his gratitude that he had not had to take Kilkenny by storm, "we must have had a new work . . . which might have cost much blood and time . . . we look at it as a gracious mercy that we have the place for you upon these terms".

Cantwell Castle, now Sandford's Court, near Kilkenny, "very strong . . . situated in a bog" was surrendered at this time. Colonel Abbot had captured Ennisnag "where were gotten a company of rogues which had revolted from Colonel Jones"; the officers were hanged, but the soldiers were granted their lives. General Sadler battered and stormed Pulkerry, near Clonmel. When the garrison continued to be "obstinate", Sadler drove them into a wooden tower and set fire to it! He also occupied Ballopoin.

Reporting these successes Cromwell reiterated his complaints about money, "I may not be wanting to tell you, and renew it again, That our hardships are not a few; . . . if moneys be not supplied, we shall not be able to carry on your work: But if it be supplied, and that speedily, I hope . . . it will not be long before England will be at an end of this charge. Sir, our horse have not had one month's pay of five. We strain what we can that the foot may be paid, or else they would starve. Those Towns that are to be reduced . . . would cost you more money that this Army hath had since we came over. I hope . . . they will come cheaper to you. I think I need not say a speedy period put to this work will break the expectation of all your enemies." He also complained that only 2,000 out of 5,000 recruits promised had been sent over to him.

Although the Scots had been the devoted allies of parliament, they disapproved of King Charles I's execution and had proclaimed his son Charles II; although they detested the Irish, they did not agree with the way they were being treated, and now they were very restive. By the beginning of 1650 parliament decided to recall their victorious general. On 8 January the House of Commons resolved that Cromwell should attend their meetings, and Lenthall wrote to him accordingly. Due to various delays the letter did not reach Oliver until 22 March. He acknowledged its receipt on 2 April, explained the delay and enquired if it still represented their will. It did, and the frigate *President Bradshaw* was ordered from Milford Haven at the end of April to bring Cromwell home.

After the capture of Kilkenny, Broghill became aware of Irish activity in Kerry. Leaving a small party to watch Limerick, he moved rapidly up the valley of the river Lee to intercept a large Irish force at Macroom, twenty-four miles west of Cork. He attacked at once, and routed the Irish, capturing Boetius Egan, Catholic bishop of New Ross. Egan was sent to Carrigadroghid and offered his life if he would persuade the Irish garrison to surrender; either he or they refused, and the bishop was hanged. But the constancy of the priest was unavailing, because hunger compelled the garrison to submit a few days later.

Continued parliamentary success made Ormonde's position more and more difficult. His Protestant troops were specially distrusted by the Catholics, and Cromwell began a series of secret negotiations to exploit this. Two emissaries, Captain Daniel and Dean Boyle, reached his headquarters, and on 16 April they signed a convention by which all Protestants, soldiers and civilians, could go to English-held Ireland or abroad. If they had any property they might have to assist in paying for the war, but otherwise, and until parliament ordered differently, they might keep their estates. Although great efforts were made to persuade both Ormonde and Inchiquin to accept these terms, they failed; but by July Ormonde had only Catholic troops upon whom he could rely.

When O'Ferrall had left Waterford, he had gone to Belturbet in County Cavan, where the Ulster chiefs had assembled to elect Owen Roe's successor. After long argument, Emer MacMahon, the Bishop of Clogher was chosen. This did not appeal to Ormonde as the prelate was one of the original conspirators of 1641; but the Ulster people were unlikely to obey anyone else. This election, too, was the last straw for General Munro and his Scots; they had been holding aloof from the fighting in the rest of Ireland, while they occupied most of Fermanagh. Now they resolved to make peace with the English Parliament. Munro accordingly made contact with Colonel Venables, and an Ironside garrison was admitted to Enniskillen. They were welcomed with great enthusiasm; at long last the tide of disorder had receded from the town's doorstep, and their courage and constancy was justified, for the Parliament of England had not forgotten them.

Cromwell's last action in Ireland was the storm of Clonmel, which represented the last irritant to be reduced before the siege of Waterford could be pressed. Clonmel was thirty miles upstream on the Suir, astride the road from Youghal to Kilkenny and covering the gap to the east of the Knockmealdown Mountains. It was far too close to Cahir, Fethard and Carrick-on-Suir, and was not out of range of Tipperary where Inchiquin had an advanced post. Covered by bad weather and darkness a capable cavalry commander should have been able to reinforce Clonmel, but such did not exist in Munster, and the garrison were left with only their own courage. It was defended by Hugh O'Neill, Owen Roe's brother, and 2,000 Ulster infantry, the best left in Ormonde's array. At the beginning of May Cromwell began to concentrate his forces round the place, and sited his artillery. O'Neill asked Ormonde for help, and Lord Castleconnel was sent with 400 reinforcements, but these arrived too late. After his request for surrender had been refused, Cromwell's guns opened fire. On 9 May a breach appeared in the walls, through which Cromwell ordered his troops to break into the town. The first attempt failed dismally; at the second the Ironsides carried the breach, but found "double-works and traverses", where very heavy fighting took place. Before they could break through these defences, darkness supervened, and Cromwell called his men back. Hugh knew that he could not hold out for a further day. Telling the townspeople to make the best terms they could, Hugh led his troops through a gap in the English lines and made for Waterford. In the morning the townspeople asked for terms, which were granted, and Cromwell entered the town in triumph, but he found O'Neill had gone. A detachment of cavalry were sent in pursuit and they managed to kill off about 200 stragglers, but the main body had got away safely. The Ironsides acknowledged that these Ulstermen were "the stoutest enemy they had ever met in Ireland".

Henry Ireton was now appointed as the Lord Deputy with orders to reduce first Waterford and then Limerick, to maintain the high standards of discipline among the English troops, and to get rid of his prisoners as fast as he could. If these latter were officers and war crimes could be proved against them they were to be shot; others and the rank and file were to be encouraged to go abroad, so that the only soldiers left in Ireland would be the hardened veterans of Cromwell. By this policy upwards of 45,000 "kurisees", as these Irish troops were called, left their native land, never to return, but to bestow upon it a celebrated renown for military virtues.

On 26 May 1650 Oliver Cromwell embarked on the frigate *President Bradshaw*, and after a rough passage arrived at Bristol five days later. His return was that of the conquering hero; the achievements in Ireland in the past nine months had been his; he had trained and led the troops; his was the strategy, his the tactics; and the great victories were especially his. Already in February Parliament had voted Cromwell the life rent of the King's property around Whitehall; now they added lands worth £2,500 a year. General Fairfax paraded the army on Hounslow Heath to give their greatest officer a ceremonial welcome on 1 June. Two days later the City of London bestowed its accolade upon him, and finally Parliament thanked him in person.

Meanwhile Bishop MacMahon was preparing to demonstrate his military ability. He realized that Coote in Derry and Venables at Coleraine were too far apart for mutual support. With true military skill Emer decided to place himself between these two, and then attack them separately. Coote had been preparing to besiege Charlemont when suddenly Emer passed to the west of Lough Neagh and fell upon Toome, where the river Bann drains that lake. This was a brilliant raid, but its success went to Emer's

head. He summoned a Council of War at Loughgall in County
Armagh, where the next move was discussed. There were three
options: they could turn on Belfast as the occupation of Toome
would give them protection; they could close on Derry; or they
could return to the safety of counties Cavan and Monaghan.
They decided on the second course, and the militant prelate
marched immediately north to Dungiven, an earth fort about
twenty miles from Derry defended by Colonel Beresford and
fifty men. They refused to surrender to Emer's summons. Dungiven was assaulted, and after a furious fight the Irish broke in
and slaughtered the garrison. This further confirmed the bishop
in his confidence. He turned north-east to seize Ballycastle
without loss. But he had outrun his communications and he had
to return at the beginning of June. Moving slowly through the
mountains, encumbered by booty, Emer traversed County Derry
to cross the river Foyle a little below Strabane. Coote hoped to
catch Emer here, but he was given the slip. Emer with his whole
force of 4,000 infantry and 400 cavalry now stood on the west bank
of the Foyle. He turned south and captured Lifford after a sharp
fight with one of Coote's patrols; but his opponents were closing
in on him, and this was the summit of his success.

Coote had been reinforced by 1,000 infantry from Belfast and
500 from Enniskillen so that by mid-June his numbers equalled
those of Emer, but his equipment was infinitely superior and his
supply situation was satisfactory. There were again three options
open to Emer: he could stay where he was; he could retire into the
hills of County Donegal; or he could make his way south-
westwards to cross the river Erne and regain the safety of Connaught or South Ulster. The first option would be difficult because
the Scottish settlers in his immediate rear were driving their cattle
into the safety of Derry or the peninsula of Inishowen, and thus
depriving Emer of the facilities for feeding his men. The third
option would require fast marching to get clear of Coote's cavalry
and to cross the Erne without being brought to battle; it would
also mean that he would have to abandon his booty. But even the
second alternative required prompt action, and in his failure to
act quickly is to be found his doom.

In the middle of June Emer sent off a substantial force to capture Doagh, a distant fortress on the Atlantic coast, some twenty-

five miles from Derry. He then sent off other parties to forage in the neighbourhood, and set off himself to Letterkenny. Here he took up a position near Scarrifhollis on a hillside overlooking the road on the western shore of Lough Swilly and protected by a large bog. Here he awaited Coote. He was advised by his professional officers either to take to the hills or to stay put, but he thought he knew better. On the arrival of Coote, Emer ordered his men down into some bad ground and began the fight. Coote also attacked, and after an hour's fighting, the Irish broke. The English cavalry was then ordered to pursue the flying Irish and the bulk of the infantry were hunted down and killed. They included Henry O'Neill, Owen's only son, and most of the professional officers who had held that army together. Sir Phelim O'Neill with a small party was lucky to reach Charlemont. The bishop escaped with an escort of 200 horse, but they were caught exhausted near Enniskillen; Emer was sent back to Derry where he was promptly hanged. "Now observe the sequel of making the Bishop a general that was nothing experienced in that lesson, nor becoming his coat to send men to spill Christian blood; and how that for want of conduct and prudency in martial affairs he lost himself and that Army that never got a foil before he led them." With Emer the last Irish field army of any size and ability had gone; and the hard core of experienced officers who might have formed the nucleus of another had been destroyed.

When Hugh O'Neill reached Waterford after the fall of Clonmel, he had quarrelled with General Preston, and as a result he had set off again with his horse to Limerick, where the townspeople implored him to take command of their defence. Already the English noose was being drawn around the town. Kilrush and Tarbert, fishing villages thirty miles down the Shannon Estuary, had been occupied by the Ironsides, and the Parliamentary Navy effectively prevented access to counties Clare and Kerry. Before beseiging Limerick, however, Ireton intended to eliminate some pockets of local Irish resistance in the rest of Ireland.

The first of these small pockets to fall was Teocroghan, a fortified country house a few miles from Trim. Colonel Reynolds with a part of the Dublin garrison had been watching the place since the late spring and it was reaching the end of its tether. To stiffen its resistance, however, Clanricarde assembled a force of 2,000 foot and 700 horse at Tyrrellspass, twenty-five miles away. Castlehaven wished to escort a supply convoy across a difficult bog, and offered to do so, if the cavalry would divert Reynold's attention. Clanricarde agreed. The last few miles of the approach march was along a narrow causeway in the heart of the bog; here Captain Fox, commanding the rear guard, faced about to protect the convoy from any possible attack from the rear; Castlehaven went on and reached Teocroghan safely, but the supplies had stayed with Fox. Castlehaven had great difficulty in getting back, and a bitter quarrel with Fox resulted with the latter being court-martialled for cowardice and shot. The attempt to relieve Teocroghan failed, and it surrendered on 25 June.

Ireton now turned on Carlow. He summoned the garrison on 2 July. Although they were greatly disheartened by the news of Teocroghan and Scarrifhollis, they held out until Sir Hardress Waller captured a tower which covered the bridge across the river Barrow; further resistance was pointless and they surrendered on 24 July.

Ireton now took direct command of the siege of Waterford. He offered the garrison fair terms, but they were rejected; so Ireton tightened up his blockade, and distress in the city became unendurable. At the end of July they asked for terms, and finally on 10 August they surrendered. Ireton reported "there marched out about 700 men, well armed, the townsmen more numerous than before we believed, and the town better fortified in all parts and more difficult to be attempted than our forces conceived, there being many stores sufficient to have maintained them a long time".

Just before the fall of Waterford, an inhabitant named Murphy left the town to make his way to the safety of the countryside; he took £80 in gold in his pocket, but he was stopped by an Ironside picquet, by whom he was killed and robbed. Two officers were involved in this. When he heard about it Ireton had them court-martialled and shot. Just because Oliver had left Ireland it was not to be assumed that standards of discipline and behaviour would be relaxed.

The little outpost at Duncannon had now lost its purpose, and when the garrison were offered the same terms as Waterford, they accepted. On 17 August Waterford Harbour was opened to the English.

After hunting down the fugitives from Scarrifhollis, Coote joined Venables to reduce Charlemont. For five weeks their combined artillery bombarded the castle, before producing a sizeable breach. Coote called upon Sir Phelim to surrender: Sir Phelim refused. Thereupon Coote ordered his men to storm the place. A really furious fight ensued; the women and children of the besieged joined in, assailing the English with hot slops and ashes; yet at the end of the day, the Irish were still in possession of all the defences. Coote had a total casualty list of over 500, but O'Neill was in an even worse plight with only thirty men capable of duty left out of an original 150. The following morning he asked for terms, which were granted. The last Ulster fortress thus fell into the hands of the English Parliament. Sir Phelim was given permission to go abroad, but he did not avail himself of this at the time; afterwards it was too late.

Before pressing the siege of Limerick, Ireton decided to lead his troops in a triumphal march across central Ireland. He intended that their passage across the land should serve as a warning to any who contemplated resistance that it would be wise to think again. In the middle of August he left Waterford for Carlow, where he struck up into the foothills of the Wicklow Mountains, an area renowned for harbouring dissidents and the disorderly; but his presence provoked those outrages he intended to suppress. As a result he had to spend a fortnight in the area harrying such as he could not catch. It was September before he reached Naas, where he decided it was safe to divide his force. Sir Hardress Waller was sent direct to Limerick while Ireton intended to cross the Shannon at Athlone and join Waller at Limerick before the month was out. Waller covered the hundred miles to Limerick in a week, demanded its surrender, which was refused, and began to besiege the place.

After treating the outlying areas of the Pale to the sight of his men, Ireton passed through Mullingar and Ballymore to arrive outside Athlone on 16 September. He had been in touch with Lord Dillon who defended the place and he hoped that Athlone would be surrendered quietly. Ormonde knew of these letters that had passed, and approved of Dillon's actions; now Ireton found himself in a very awkward position. He found that Athlone was hostile, and he could not storm it without his artillery, which was still near Waterford; he could not cross the Shannon, for the only bridge was in Athlone; he had been successfully hoodwinked! Leaving Coote to watch the town, and Colonel Axtel to garrison King's County, Ireton made his way down the east bank of the Shannon to reach Limerick on 6 October. He, too, summoned O'Neill to surrender, and again was refused. It was too late in the year to press the siege, and Ireton could only leave sufficient troops to contain any break-out before recommencing the siege in the following spring.

But if the failure of the Limerick operation was a nuisance to Ireton, Ormonde's authority, already weakened by defeat and wasted by desertion, was to be dissipated by two cruel political blows. The Clonmacnoise prelates had met again at Loughrea that summer to press the claims of the Catholic Church; Ormonde had merely noted their opinions. Dissatisfied with this, they met again at Jamestown in County Leitrim. Pointing out to Ormonde that he had neither an army nor money, that the English were taxing the Irish to pay for the war "so that we are in a fair way for losing our sacred religion, the King's authority, and Ireland", they invited him to be present at their meetings. Feeling that this could only lead to quarrels, he refused, so on 12 August, the prelates excommunicated Ormonde's adherents, and demanded that he quit Ireland and appoint a Catholic deputy. Ormonde ignored them, but the harm had been done.

In the summer of 1650 King Charles II made his way to Scotland. The conditions exacted by his countrymen for his restoration to his other thrones were very unpleasant to this sophisticated young man. He had to adhere to the strict Calvinistic doctrines of their Kirk; he was in a cleft stick, since he could neither return to the Continent nor reject their demands. On 16 August 1650 at Dunfermline he signed a declaration acknowledging his own and his parents' sins in opposing the Covenant and permitting any tolerance to Catholics. He was obliged to admit his "exceeding great sinfulness . . . of that treaty and peace made with the bloody Irish rebels, who treacherously shed the blood of so many of his faithful and loyal subjects in Ireland"; and he had to revoke the commissions he had granted. This was a disgraceful act, and King Charles II tried to avoid the consequences of his own moral cowardice. The Dean of Tuam, who had taken refuge in Scotland, was summoned to the King's presence. The King complained, "The Scots have dealt very ill with me. I have been forced to do some things which may much prejudice [Lord Ormonde]." The Dean was then sent to Ireland to explain the situation to the Lord Lieutenant.

He left Dunfermline at the end of August and after a long and dangerous journey he reached Ormonde on 13 October. The contents of the Dunfermline Declaration had been regarded by Ormonde as lying propaganda, but now there was no room left for doubt. Ormonde accordingly asked the Commissioners of Trust to meet him at Ennis on 23 October and as a result of this meeting he convoked an assembly at Loughrea on 15 November. He explained the situation as reported by the Dean of Tuam, and then announced that he regarded the Dunfermline declaration as invalid until the Irish nation had "free and safe access unto His Majesty, provided the Jamestown excommunications were revoked". In the discussions which followed, dissension soon arose which Ormonde brought to an end by announcing that he intended to leave Ireland. On 7 December they suddenly stopped their quarrels and reached agreement: the episcopacy said they would not usurp the Royal authority and were only concerned with the preservation of the Catholic religion; the nobility and the gentry agreed that the Royal authority was the only satisfactory bond of unity; all asked Ormonde to appoint a suitable deputy and thanked him for risking everything in the cause of his duty to Ireland. This reached Ormonde at Geneinagh, a little port in Clare, where he was preparing to leave. He then issued a commission as deputy to Lord Clanricarde, the only possible person who was trusted, and issued certain parting instructions about his duty. He then left in a fast sloop of four guns on 11 December; with him went Inchiquin, Daniel O'Neill, Richard Belling, and some other senior officers. Twelve years were to pass before they saw Ireland again.

In mid-October Sir Charles Coote realized he had no hope of capturing Athlone that winter, so he withdrew to Derry, making a wide sweep to avoid being caught at a disadvantage in the swamps and bogs on the direct route. At the same time Axtel set off with 800 men from Kilkenny to visit his garrisons in King's County. Clanricarde also had interests there, because the small posts were inadequately supported. He crossed the Shannon with over 3,000 men, and moved rapidly south from Athlone. He captured Ferbane without difficulty and laid siege to Kilcolgan. When Axtel reached this vicinity he knew that he was in the presence of a greatly superior force; he sent for help, and withdrew towards Roscrea. Clanricarde followed him up, taking Birr and Streamstown on the way. Help reached Axtel at Roscrea, and he turned on Clanricarde, who retired just as promptly. Abandoning Birr the Irish retreated on to Meelick Island in the Shannon near Banagher. On 25 October Axtel found them there and sent his men along a causeway which gave access to the Irish position. At the neck of the approach the Irish had prepared a defensive position which they held tenaciously; after a long and bloody struggle, however, Axtel's men broke through the defences and killed all but some 300 Irishmen who managed to swim the Shannon. Clanricarde was absent on this occasion, but he lost all his own baggage. His remaining posts east of the Shannon were hurriedly abandoned, and the troops made their way to Connaught.

Ireton had been investing Nenagh without much success, but as a result of this victory Axtel was able to send him a substantial reinforcement, and the town surrendered on 30 October. The main body of the Ironsides were then marched back to Kilkenny, and only outposts remained in contact with the Irish through the rest of the winter. In his six months of supreme command, Ireton had achieved much, and had lost little, but the speed of his acquisitions bore little resemblance to the rapid master strokes of his father-in-law.

The turmoil and strife which had disturbed the British Isles over the past twelve years had been watched by many of the turbulent nobles of Europe with covetous eyes, in the hope of some rich pickings at small cost. One of these was Charles IV, Duke of Lorraine; he was at once a bad statesman and a competent soldier, both mean and dishonest. He wanted his cake and to eat it too. He began life by losing his duchy, but he had recouped his loss by indiscriminate looting, and was prepared to reinvest his fortune in another market. In the Irish troubles, men were wondering if the Stuarts were the best family to preside over their affairs. Ireland and Duke Charles were thus thrown in each other's way. The Clonmacnoise assembly sent the Duke a formal request for aid in December 1649, and for the next three years negotiations continued; but their very existence sapped the life out of Irish resistance. They always hoped, Micawber-like, to receive substantial assistance; it never came. The Irish began by offering Duncannon as a security for a loan of £24,000; but before the deal could be clinched, Ireton had Duncannon. Galway was then offered, but mutual distrust prevented agreement. Finally after a lot of hard and astute bargaining, with the security of both Galway and Limerick, Duke Charles did lend £20,000, but gross dishonesty filched £6,000 before it reached the Irish! Ormonde thought the duke was throwing away good money, and that the Irish were purchasing slavery, "the frequent lot of such as affect immoderate power upon weak foundations".

The English Parliament was well informed about all these dealings. Their spies in Ireland provided timely information on the one hand. While Cardinal Mazarin was far more interested in the positive friendship of the Commonwealth than the ephemeral blessings of universal Catholicism, he filled in all the other details for the English on the other hand. As a result of their intelligence the English could afford to regard the whole negotiations with cynical contempt; nothing could stop their continued and remorseless advance. They were so confident of the outcome that they ushered in the New Year of 1651 by reducing the monthly maintenance grant for the troops from £33,000 to £20,000; and they were fully justified in thinking that the prosperity of reoccupied Ireland could sustain the additional taxation.

In the spring of 1651 Clanricarde tried to reconstitute the Irish forces of O'Neill and Preston in Westmeath, Cavan and Longford. Hewson and Reynolds were ordered to prevent this. In mid-March Reynolds stormed Donore, killing the garrison and seizing a vast stock of corn. Hewson left Teocroghan on 14 March and captured Kilbride three days later. These two then repaired and garrisoned Ballymore, and then turned north-east to capture Ballinalack. The Irish at Finnea, between Loughs Kinale and Sheelin, put up a stout fight and had to be blockaded. They were supported by Lord Westmeath at Termonbarry in County Roscommon, and Phil O'Reilly in the adjacent village of Togher. Hewson advanced towards these places. He surprised O'Reilly one morning after his troops had engaged in a heavy drinking session the previous evening. O'Reilly was lucky to escape, but over forty officers and 400 rank and file were captured; they were sent under strong guard to Dublin to await shipment to the West Indies. As all hope of relief was destroyed, Finnea surrendered.

In April Coote was ordered to advance from Ulster along the Atlantic coast to Sligo, and then to cross to Galway; Reynolds went with some cavalry to assist him. The Irish were unable to resist, and at the end of May these two entered Athenry. Two days later they passed through Loughrea, and went on to Portumna on the Shannon. Meanwhile Hewson had closed round Athlone. These movements diverted Clanricarde's attention from Ireton, who left Kilkenny in April to press the siege of Limerick. Learning that Castlehaven covered the Shannon crossing at Killaloe, he marched there. He then offered the nobleman personal terms. Ireton pointed out that Castlehaven's position was ultimately hopeless, but he could, if he gave in now, go and settle quietly on his estate in England; the alternative was probably death and certainly deprivation of all his property. The offer was rejected and Ireton prepared to cross the Shannon at Killaloe, at O'Brien's Bridge and at Castleconnell. On 2 June a surprise crossing at O'Brien's Bridge took 500 men across the river in an hour; the party watching the Castleconnell bridge site was withdrawn to drive in the O'Brien's Bridge crossing, whereupon Colonel Ingoldsby with 300 cavalry crossed unopposed at Castleconnell and took the defenders at O'Brien's Bridge in the rear. This caused a panic among the Irish, who abandoned their positions; the force at Killaloe followed suit and retired upon Limerick. Castlehaven himself went north to join Clanricarde at Loughrea.

Learning that Coote was very near Portumna, Ireton now sent Ludlow with 1,000 horse to join him. This party made its way along the desolated western shores of Lough Derg. The country was almost devoid of inhabitants, and during their forty mile ride they only met one encampment of six families who led a wandering existence following their herds. He left the bulk of his men some miles short of Portumna and hurried on with a small party to assist in its reduction. The appearance of yet more English persuaded the garrison to surrender the next morning. Ludlow and Coote now set off in pursuit of Clanricarde, whom they chased as far as Ballinasloe; rather than stand an English attack the town surrendered, and a small garrison was left there. Reynolds returned to Portumna, and Ludlow marched back to Limerick; on the way he subdued an Irish force at Gort, and also rounded up 500 head of cattle to help feed Ireton's camp.

Meanwhile Ireton had turned south towards Limerick. He drove in an Irish picquet at Ferboe on 3 June, and Colonel Ingoldsby pursued them to Thomond Bridge where 150 were killed or drowned. The English Navy now began landing stores and artillery in the Shannon Estuary; as the lower reaches were already garrisoned by Ironsides it was possible to maintain the troops outside Limerick by water. Ireton was ready to reduce the town by shelling on 19 June so he summoned O'Neill to surrender. When he refused, 28 guns opened on the Castle covering Thomond Bridge; and Ireton's mortars harrassed the town itself. A great salmon weir crossed the Shannon just above Thomond Bridge, and across it Ireton formed a bridgehead on 20 June; the Castle which had been built to guard against this very contingency was destroyed by the mortars and the garrison was captured as they fled.

Ireton's sappers built a substantial wooden bridge across the Shannon at Castleconnell, which enabled the Lord Deputy to move troops into Connaught with ease, and to supply his investing forces on the west shore at Limerick. They also built a floating bridge just downstream of the beleaguered city, and this enabled Ireton to switch his troops tactically; as soon as it was completed the Clare end was fortified, and the bulk of the English forces were moved across. They now successfully stormed the Thomond Bridge Castle, but they could not break into the town. Ireton then tried to seize the upper end of King's Island, on the lower end of which stood the bulk of the city of Limerick. Five boatloads of troops were quietly landed before the Irish knew what was happening; but when they did, O'Neill launched a successful counter-attack, killing about 90 English.

Muskerry still had about 5,000 men distributed in County Kerry: John Fitzpatrick had a remnant of Leinster men at Galbally, just south-west of Tipperary. They were about 50 miles apart, and swift movement could effect their junction. But they missed their opportunity when a diversion occurred in County

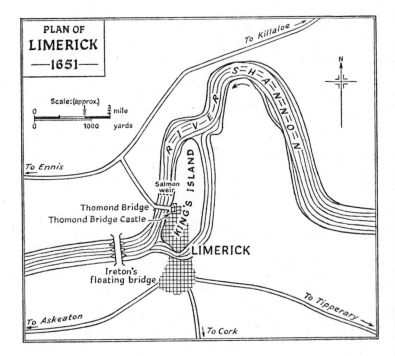

During the siege of Limerick Ireton's troops were principally divided between a small area just West of Thomond Bridge and an encampment adjacent to the Cork road, South of the City.

Clare. The English suddenly captured Carrigaholt by surprise; then Roche with about 3,000 Irish troops besieged them; Ludlow was sent to break up the Irish concentration. He left Limerick at the end of June, crossed the river Fergus near Ennis; but Roche and he missed each other. The garrison at Carrigaholt took the opportunity to evacuate the place and return to the English lines. Finally Ludlow came upon Roche at Inchcronan, and defeated him; the Irish were sufficiently nimble, however, to avoid pursuit in the woods and swamps. After this Broghill set off to intercept Muskerry with a force of 600 foot and 400 horse.

Muskerry had collected nearly 3,000 troops and assembled them near Drishane. He crossed the Blackwater and reached Dromagh without incident. Broghill, at Castlelyons, now learnt of Muskerry's moves and he marched to Mallow on 21 July. The following day in very bad weather he reached the Irish outposts at Castleishin. Muskerry promptly withdrew to Dromagh, and then to Drishane. The heavy rains prevented Broghill from following, and he returned to Mallow for supplies. After this Broghill moved westwards to look for Fitzpatrick, but between Banteer and Kanturk, Muskerry ambushed him. Broghill was in the river valley and Muskerry on the hill tops. Instead of staying where they were, the Irish charged down the hillsides, and attacked; discipline saved the English, and at the end of a long and exhausting struggle they escaped. Broghill was badly shaken by this; but Muskerry had fought the last pitched battle of the war, and was so exhausted that he could not reform his forces.

At the beginning of August Fitzpatrick found the English garrison at Meelick asleep, and he killed them. On 5 August Phil O'Reilly attacked Finnea, but he was driven off with great loss. Even in Dublin 2,000 men had to be kept ready to intercept Sir John Sherlock who lay hidden in the Wicklow Hills with a determined band of Irishmen. The Fabian tactics of the Irish could only be combatted by an increase in the English field forces, which were tied down outside Limerick, so Ireton redoubled his efforts to reduce the city in August.

Roche had sent a message into Limerick by a country woman; she was, however, caught by the Ironsides and hanged "for fear of giving further intelligence". O'Neill wished to get rid of every useless mouth in the town, and he encouraged such as wished to try and leave; very few succeeded, and those who failed were hanged by the English. By the end of September Ireton obtained a reinforcement of guns, which he promptly brought into action. This was the signal for the end; there were two factions in the town, and those who wished to see it out to the bitter end were voted down. On 27 October Limerick surrendered. The original garrison of 2,000 had been reduced to 1,200, and over 5,000 townspeople had lost their lives either in battle or from the effects of the plague which had just started to erupt. Most of the soldiers and the townspeople were allowed to disperse with what they could carry; but some of the irreconcilable officers, such as General Purcell and the Bishop of Emly, were put to death, generally for the outrages they had committed in 1641.

After the fall of Limerick Ireton and Ludlow began to suppress the remaining Irish resistance in County Clare. On 4 November Clare Castle surrendered; the garrison were permitted to disperse. They went on to the barony of Burren where "there is not water enough to drown a man, wood enough to hang one, nor earth enough to bury him". The weather was frightful, and both generals developed bad colds. For Ireton, exhausted by worry, this was the last straw; he reached Limerick on his return, but on 26 November he died. His body was embalmed, taken back to England, and given a State Funeral in Westminster Abbey. As he had signed the King's death-warrant, his body was exhumed at the Restoration. Ireton was a capable officer with a very high sense of duty; he insisted on his orders being strictly obeyed, and he had in addition a strong sense of humanity. Just before he died he learnt that Colonel Axtel had permitted some prisoners to be killed after one of his officers had admitted them to quarter; even although Axtel knew nothing of the facts before the deed was done, Ireton relieved him of his command and sent him home.

Ludlow was now appointed Commander-in-Chief of the army, and his task was the steady reduction of the remaining Irish fortresses and the elimination of the swamp-dwelling banditry. He summoned his senior officers to meet him at Kilkenny just before Christmas and he explained his plan. This was to create protected areas, inside which life would be normal and where only English and "obedient" Irish might live; outside these areas he would destroy all means of subsistence.

His first protected area was to be an extended Pale enclosed by the rivers Boyne and Barrow but excluding the Wicklow Hills. Here no smith, harness-maker or armourer would be allowed outside an English garrison; nor would strong drink, or any market be permitted beyond these limits.

Up in the Wicklow Mountains the peasantry had been running with the hare and hunting with the hounds. The strict policy of the English in paying for supplies had produced prosperity; the presence of priests and bandits who could melt into the hills provided that element of excitement inseparable from life in Ireland. This was natural for they sympathized with their own soldiers, defeated but not yet subdued, and when the Ironsides came to suppress disorder, they made money! At the end of February 1652 Ludlow posted a strong garrison at Talbotstown, and then began to comb through the Wicklow Hills, destroying all means of subsistence and subjecting every Irishman he could catch to rigorous interrogation. Few were caught, but he harried the valleys, pulling down every building he could and carrying off every particle of food he could find. This scourging of the land severely restricted the capacity of the Irish to resist.

As in Limerick so in Galway there were two factions in the town; here, however, the fear of the commander of the besiegers, Sir Charles Coote, who owned a substantial estate in Connaught, was a potent factor in inducing the townspeople to ask for terms. On 12 May, Coote granted these and they included a guarantee against pillage and violence with quarter for the garrison. When Ludlow read the terms, he ordered Coote to stiffen them up, but by now Galway had surrendered. Coote apologized to the townspeople for having to stiffen the conditions, but he pointed out that if they both had not agreed when they did, far greater suffering would have resulted.

Clanricarde now had virtually no base, and King Charles II gave him permission to leave Ireland when he could no longer resist. After a very bold raid into Donegal, and slipping through the net spread for him by Coote and Venables, Clanricarde was finally surrounded in the island of Carrick. Rather than face the consequences of pointless resistance, he surrendered on 28 June, and he was allowed to retire to his English estate at Somerhill in Kent.

Muskerry was still at large in County Kerry, where his chief stronghold was Ross Castle, on an island in the lower lake of Killarney. In June Dromagh had surrendered and this enabled Ludlow and Broghill to approach Ross with 4,000 infantry and 2,000 cavalry. They found that the garrison was being supplied by the country-people from the opposite side of the lake by water; to stop this would require shipping on the lake and vigorous cavalry patrolling round the shores. A frigate was therefore sent from Cork, with a string of barges, to Castlemaine Harbour and these were dragged laboriously up the river Laune. Before this could be done a party of Irish had to be thrown out of Killagh Abbey at the mouth of the river. Two of the largest barges were sent overland from Kinsale and reassembled on the lake! On 20 June the whole armada was assembled on the lake under Captain Chudleigh, a parliamentary seaman who had risen to high rank by sheer ability. These preparations turned out to be unnecessary, for negotiations for a major surrender were now completed. Lord Westmeath agreed to his troops of 11 infantry and 6 cavalry regiments laying down their arms at Mullingar, Maryborough, Carlow and Kildare on 1 June on quite generous terms. On hearing of this Muskerry in Ross agreed to order the capitulation of all his men, amounting to 960 in the castle and more than 3,000 elsewhere in Kerry.

The war was now virtually over. Various parties of Irish continued to resist, or avoided surrender for some time yet to come. The English commanders were no longer concerned with positive resistance, but with completing the pacification of Ireland by disarming what was left of their opponents, and when they cornered parties of Irish lenient conditions were generally offered. In the late summer Charles Fleetwood, who had just married Ireton's widow, was appointed to the command of the army in Ireland, superseding Ludlow who returned to England shortly afterwards.

In February Inishbofin Island surrendered on the usual terms. Roger Moore, one of the original authors of the 1641 rising, was there, but he avoided notice and made his way to Ulster where he lived out his days in seclusion as a fisherman. On 27 April 1653 the very last post, Cloughoughter, surrendered; this had been held by Phil O'Reilly, who was given permission to go abroad, and he was wise enough to avail himself of this.

Peace had returned to Ireland. For nearly twelve years bloodshed had disgraced the Emerald Isle; now, after a terrible struggle, the last remnant of Irish resistance had been brought to an end. The Parliament of England was the undisputed victor; they had won the war; could they impose upon Ireland a lasting peace?

The primary source for the initial campaign in the south of Ireland is Cromwell's own letters and reports. This includes his correspondence with Col. David Sinnot at Wexford, Lucas Taafe at New Ross, and other Irish commanders, the details of the Clonmacnoise Manifestoes, and Cromwell's reply, as well as numerous letters to Lenthall and his own family.

Much detail can be obtained from Bagwell, D'Alton and Gilbert, as well as:

M. Ashley: *Cromwell's Generals.*
S. R. Gardiner: *History of the Commonwealth and Protectorate* (1901).
R. W. Ramsay: *Henry Ireton* (1949).

CHAPTER 7

The Settlement

IRELAND now lay helpless beneath the mailed fist of Oliver Cromwell and the Puritans of England: they were her conquerors, their rights had been established by the supreme authority of the sword. Their doctrines were simple; their objects were plain; their policies were obvious. They would complete the work upon which the English and the Scottish peoples had resolved twelve years before; which, due to their own internecine strife, they had been unable to consummate until now; and which, due to the outstanding ability of their military commanders, now lay absolutely in the hollow of their hands. Crushed by overwhelming military might; oppressed by their sense of failure, distracted by futile quarrels over the causes of their defeat, rejected by the Catholic powers of Europe, apprehensive of reprisals, the Irish could only wait for the details of the doom which their new masters would shortly pronounce upon them.

Basically there were six separate problems. The original adventurers wanted to be put into possession of the estates they had bought many years before; the Ironsides wanted the arrears of their pay, the rewards of their risks and hardships; the English people and the loyalists wanted to hear that exemplary punishment had been meted out to such perpetrators of atrocities as could be caught; the new Government of Ireland wished to be rid of the defeated and disbanded Irish soldiers who might so easily rise in arms again; the original colonists wanted some reward for their loyalty or timely conversion and the new ones wanted a secure settlement; and the Puritans intended that the

Catholic religion should be eliminated for all time from the Irish scene. These problems were all connected and each depended upon the vigour and zeal with which the complementary policies were executed.

By the original Act of the Long Parliament dated 19 March 1642 passed to suppress the 1641 rising, 2,500,000 acres of Ireland were declared forfeit, and these were offered for sale to whoever would "adventure" his money on such a hazard at the rate of £200 for every 1,000 acres in Ulster, £300 for the same in Connaught, £450 in Munster and £600 in Leinster. Debentures were issued to be redeemed after the suppression of the rising. The Act was soon amended to allow Scots and Dutch Protestants to subscribe as well as Englishmen, provided they did so before 10 May 1642. It was amended again to permit those who bought their debentures before 20 July 1642 to have their land measured in Irish acres of 7,231 square yards instead of English acres of 4,840 square yards. But the most important change was the Doubling Ordnance of 14 July 1643; this invited existing debenture holders to subscribe a further quarter of the price they had already paid in return for doubling their allocation of land. By this time the pay arrears of the parliamentary army were rising to unmanageable heights. To extinguish these obligations, officers were permitted to purchase debentures with their unpaid arrears. In these ways £294,095 was subscribed and land grants of 1,038,234 acres were made. By the end of the English Civil War the sum had reached £360,000.

Before the Ironsides had embarked for Ireland in 1649 Cromwell had promised them their arrears out of the land of Ireland: they had conquered the land, and they looked upon it as theirs to parcel out among themselves. At the beginning of 1652 there were about 30,000 English troops under arms in Ireland, and their annual budget ran to about £500,000: taxation in Ireland only covered about one fifth of this, and the balance had to come from England. The arrears had now reached the enormous figure of £1,550,000, and the Council of England was anxious to discharge this for the soldiers at the same rate as the adventurers had obtained their expectations. At the same time and in the same way, the debts due for supplies and services to the army in Ireland, amounting to a further £1,750,000, were also discharged.

Although the Parliament of England was not to declare the Irish Rebellion at an end until 27 September 1653, their Commissioners in Ireland proposed on 1 January 1652 that the adventurers should cast lots for their lands immediately and that the soldiers should have land allotted to them in close proximity to their garrisons. This was to encourage the troops to cultivate the land pending its formal allocation, and to prevent the indolent garrisons becoming hot-beds of discontent. On 30 January the adventurers were called to a meeting with a committee of the House of Commons to discuss some form of speedy plantation of Ireland; the ensuing discussions went on into the middle of the following year.

Before the land could be effectively resettled there were three categories of occupier who had necessarily to be evicted. The Irish soldier who knew no other trade than the sword had often returned home after the town he had defended had surrendered or the field force in which he had served had been broken up. He knew he had lost, and that the cause was the quarrels of his leaders. When the English guard was down a new leader might summon him to arms once more, and he would not be slow to respond. The Irish Catholic priests had remained with their flocks, giving such solace as they could to the very badly battered nation, and still performing their spiritual duties as best they could. Throughout this period their very secure intelligence system provided vital information to the Irish commanders. Almost invariably exempted from protection to surrendered troops and townships, their behaviour provides a remarkable example of duty performed at the gravest risk and without regard to the dreadful consequences of discovery. Generally holding the affection of these two categories was the original proprietor of the land. It is a cardinal principal of English law that no man shall be deprived of his land except by the judgement of his peers. To deprive the instigators of the rebellion, and their principal subsequent adherents, of their land was not likely to cause difficulty; but many of the smaller landlords had supported their local troops if only to enjoy a quiet life. To prove such support which had been given in money and produce and not by personal service would be virtually hopeless. Yet this broad mass of landlords had enabled the Irish to prolong the struggle, and the

Parliament of England was determined to make them suffer for their behaviour.

During the summer of 1652 the successive surrenders of large bodies of Irish troops had contained provisions for men dissatisfied with their lot to leave the country on condition that they never bore arms against the Parliament of England. To encourage such an emigration facilities were given to foreign recruiting agents. A certain Don Ricardo White sent over 7,000 from the ports of Munster to Spain in May 1652. A Colonel Mayo took another 3,000 in September. Similar parties went to France, Poland and Italy. About 40,000 young Irishmen left the country in this way between 1651 and 1655: few ever returned.

It was felt by those concerned with the resettlement that if the laws proscribing the Catholic priesthood were strictly enforced the country might become Protestant. If there were no priests to instruct the young in Catholic doctrines, then the facilities for Protestant missionaries would be improved, and the opportunities for subversion would be diminished. But to detect priests was not so easy; £20 reward was offered for information leading to their arrest; to assist one was a capital crime. Although many were caught and either killed or transported, many more managed to evade arrest. Most took to the hills and swamps where the surviving Irish still in arms would benefit from their spiritual ministrations and provide for their essential but Spartan bodily needs. On 6 January 1653, in a great effort to entice these devoted men to leave Ireland, the government offered to allow all priests prepared to accompany Irish troops going abroad a general liberty to proceed without molestation to the waterside for embarkation. Three weeks were allowed for the priests to take advantage of the offer, after which the penal laws would be even more rigorously enforced: some took advantage of the offer, but most remained in Ireland. Five pounds was now offered to anyone lodging a priest in jail; this was a liberal reward and English troops went "priest-hunting", with substantial success. These ministers of religion were herded into jails and internment camps throughout Ireland, and were then moved progressively to the ports for shipment overseas like cattle. The general overcrowding induced the government to relent in some rare instances. A certain William Shiel was old, lame and weak;

he was allowed to reside in Connaught provided he remained within one mile of his residence and did not exercise his priestly function. Another priest, Roger Begs, was allowed four months, leave on the same conditions prior to leaving Ireland for ever. Sometimes the seizure of priests led to fighting: in November 1652 Captain Thomas Shepherd broke up a Mass being said near Old Leighlin in County Carlow. At the same time Cornet Greatrex was resisted at Baltrasna in Meath, but he arrested five of the Irish gentry and a priest.

But the sternest measures were reserved for the landed proprietors of Ireland. In what amounted to a mass Act of Attainder most of the land was brought under the direct control of parliament. "Whereas," began the Act for the Settlement of Ireland of 12 August 1652, "the Parliament of England, after the expense of much blood and treasure for the suppression of the horrid rebellion in Ireland, have by the good hand of God upon their undertakings, brought that affair to such an issue, as that a total reducement and settlement of that nation may be speedily effected, to the end that the people of that nation may know that it is not the intention of the parliament to extirpate (them), but that mercy and pardon, both as to life and estate, may be extended to all husbandmen, ploughmen, labourers, artificers and others of the inferior sort ... they submitting themselves to the Parliament of the Commonwealth of England, and living peaceably and obediently under their government; and that others of higher rank and quality may know parliament's intention concerning them, according to the respective demerits and considerations under which they fall." It proceeded to class the Irish into six categories. In the first all original rebels, defined as those in arms prior to the sitting of the first General Assembly at Kilkenny on 10 November 1642 and those who had sustained them, were excluded from pardon of life or estate. In the second the entire priesthood was enmeshed in a new proscription. The third clause denied pardon from Lords Ormonde, Castlehaven, Clanricarde, Inchiquin, Muskerry, Taafe and some others specially named. Those Irish civilians who had killed any English, and those Irish troops who had killed English civilians were condemned. The fifth clause gave the remaining Irish still in arms twenty eight days to submit, or be excluded from pardon. All senior officers of the

Irish armies were deprived of two-thirds of their land and were personally banished "during the pleasure of Parliament"; the remaining third of their estate might support their families. The seventh clause gave the Commissioners of Parliament and the Commander-in-Chief a power to extend mercy for life to soldiers, but they were to be deprived of two-thirds of their estates, and the remaining third was to be reallocated elsewhere. Then all Catholics who had "not manifested their constant good affection to the interests . . . of England" were to be deprived of one-third of their estate, and have the remainder reallocated elsewhere. All non-Catholics who fell into the same group were just deprived of a fifth part of their estate. By the ninth clause those having no real or personal estate exceeding ten pounds who would take a new oath of allegiance were to be pardoned for life and estate for any act done in the prosecution of the war.

This Ordnance of the Commonwealth is often stigmatized as being the order for the obliteration of the Irish nation. But careful examination shows that the Puritans would be content with the strict punishment of those responsible for the rebellion and the atrocities, and a heavy taxation upon those who had enabled the struggle to continue. It was not the strict expiation of the sins of the Irish upon which the victors might so easily have insisted but their very moderation which was remarkable. Usually the victors expropriated not just a portion of the property of the vanquished; they took it all, and the life of the owner too, if they could. The English would be content with less, but they ignored the harsh advice of Machiavelli: either kill your enemy or make a friend of him. This policy decision of the Commonwealth reprieved the Irishman, but the price he had to pay for his life also purchased his enmity for generations yet to come. Within the very wording of the Ordnance were to be found the seeds of its own destruction.

Initially parliament intended that Leinster should make a new and enlarged English Pale; beyond this Ulster and Munster would form a buffer region, occupied by English and "friendly" Irish; while beyond this, in the wild region of Connaught the bulk of the Irish could be contained by the sea and the river line of the Shannon.

The northern part of County Dublin and the land between Cork

and Youghal were allotted to wounded soldiers and the families
of those who had not survived. Here the land was good, the
prospects were better and the security from roaming bands of
Irish was best. In these enclaves the weak would be safe. The rest
of Counties Cork and Dublin, together with Kildare and Carlow
were reserved by the government for "special planting"; here the
friends of the English might expect to receive a fruitful reward.
The rest of the land lying to the east of the rivers Boyne and
Barrow would form the new Pale. If this prospered the government intended to plant a second Pale in County Cork to the south
of the river Blackwater. Outside these Pales a thick belt of country
was allotted to the adventurers and the soldiers jointly It was
felt that each would provide the other with mutual support; that
the presence of the Cromwellian veterans would give the civilians
that confidence necessary to sustain their new life in a potentially
hostile country. In Ulster, Antrim, Down and Armagh were thus
split; Meath, Westmeath, King's and Queen's Counties in Leinster
and Limerick, Tipperary and Waterford in Munster were similarly
divided. County Louth was reserved in its entirety for the adventurers, while the remainder of Ulster, Leinster and Munster
(other than County Clare) was given over to the army. But in
spite of this ample allocation, there was still insufficient land
available, and the soldiers' allocation was made up in Connaught
from Leitrim, Sligo and a portion of Mayo.

The rest of the Province of Connaught and County Clare were
to provide a survivors' enclave for the Irish. Delimited on the
east by the natural barrier of the Shannon, on the north-east by
the English military settlement, and elsewhere by the sea, this
whole area was to become a vast internment camp, a living Irish
hell. On the water barriers, on this new Styx, who could perform
the functions of Cerberus better than the new proprietors of the
soil, the old veterans of Cromwell? A strip of land, originally
four miles wide, but later reduced to one mile, along the Shannon
and around the Atlantic coast was specially planted with the most
zealous of the Puritan warriors, chosen particularly for their
known vigilance. Yet even inside this the Irish were to be further
constricted: a strip of five miles around Galway and the barony of
Clare stretching to Headford and Tuam were specially reserved
for an English garrison. All islands off the coast were to be cleared

of the Irish, and at the same time any English in the province were to depart with the promise of equivalent land in some other part of Ireland. Into this emasculated province the hard core of the leadership of the Irish nation were to be driven. Here were no industries capable of sustaining war, no fortresses, no ports, and no natural defences; here the Irish could expect only degradation and despair. If they started any trouble the Puritans would not hesitate for an instant to march in and suppress it with the utmost harshness.

On 26 September 1653 parliament passed the basic Ordnance "for the satisfaction of the adventurers for the lands in Ireland and Arrears due to the soldiery there". This declared that all forfeited land passed into new hands on that date, and required the old owners to move to the parts of Ireland "assigned for the habitation of the Irish nation" before 1 May 1654, or face death. The Council of Ireland were to administer the policy, and to grant the necessary waivers of the new law. Well aware of the practical difficulties of this they made what were probably the best arrangements that were possible.

In central and eastern Ireland there were many estates where the mansion was occupied by an English officer and his troops. The old proprietor with such of his tenants as remained lived in the village. Together they subsisted on what the soil would produce, and by the summer of 1653 this was starting to resemble the harvests of twelve years previously. There was still a shortage of livestock, the farm implements were worn out and could not be replaced, the facilities for marketing the surplus were rudimentary; but the country was starting to take on an air of well-being, the land was being put into good heart. It was the official view that the English troops should assist in this work, if only to keep idle hands from mischief. They were promised the rewards of their toil at harvest time. The Irish, too, had raised crops on such land as the English officer permitted them to till. Since it had increased the gross national product this had been blessed, and the surplus had been sold to enable the tax assessments to be paid. Then just after the harvest was in the Irish gentry, with their tenants and servants, were ordered to move into Connaught. The peasantry were not required to transplant because they would be useful to their new English masters as earth tillers and herdsmen; deprived, too, of their priests and the gentry they might even become Protestants.

The English officers, effectively the landlords during this period of hiatus, were deeply disturbed by these new orders. They felt that their word had been personally pledged to the Irish gentry that the fruits of their toil should not be taken away from them; they wished to keep the land sweet with the planting of winter cereal crops, and now the incentive to the Irish was being swept away. The Irish were panic-stricken at the prospect of having to travel to their new homes during the winter, and they dreaded, with reason, what they might find in Connaught. At the same time the English soldiers were too few to keep the estates running, nor could they be put into occupation of their new lands in sufficient time to sow such winter crops. The great danger was that an already wasted Ireland might lose half the following year's harvest: just as everything was taking on a new look after the long years of famine, war and disorder, all would go back into the melting pot. Already Ireland had begun to cast her special charm over her conqueror: already the conqueror's interests were those of Ireland. The English officers were able to make known their feelings to their superiors, and to bring their pressures to bear in private; their remonstrances could be made without the world at large knowing the differences between the junior officers in central Ireland and the council in Dublin.

The machinery to administer the transplantation was fairly simple. The potential transplantee was to report to the local Revenue officer with a full statement of his circumstances, his family and servants, his livestock and crops, the extent and quality of his lands and so on; this was known as his Particular. After this had been certified, he was to take it to Commissioners at Loughrea, who would set out the equivalent of land in Connaught after making the proper deduction for the forfeited part in accordance with the Ordnance of 12 August 1652. But these Commissioners were only to assign land on a temporary basis, and the final settlement was reserved for another set of Commissioners at Athlone at some future date. The orders setting out these arrangements were issued on 15 October 1653. Heads of families were to report at Loughrea before 30 January 1654, and after being allotted their appropriate patch they were to erect the necessary accommodation for their families and dependants, who were to join them before 1 May 1654. The land allocations were to be made in accordance with the livestock it would have to support, the anticipated crop which had been left behind as well as the unforfeited third, or whatever it was, that was abandoned in the east. For each acre of winter corn, three Connaught acres would be assigned, for each cow or bullock, three acres, and for every sheep one third of an acre.

As might be expected every variety of excuse was advanced by the Irish to avoid transplantation. Some said they were too sick to move, or that their wives and families could not be expected to survive the winter's journey; others said their cattle were not fit to be driven; there were claims to standing crops; there were petitions that the articles of capitulation of some place gave permission to those surrendering to return home where they could remain so long as they remained peaceable; there were some who declared they were only winding up their affairs prior to leaving Ireland for ever. After some delay, the council granted dispensation fairly liberally to the wives and children of transplantees who had actually gone to Connaught. But on 1 May, those left behind would become tenants of the new proprietor or the State, and would have to provide every fifth sheaf of the harvest for the new landlord to compensate him for this dispensation. Generally these permissions operated to relieve the harshest elements, but sometimes the local English commander saw fit to ignore the Dublin dispensations and to eject, often with great vigour, those who had been left behind and to refuse any grazing for the livestock.

As in all great upheavals of this nature opportunities were not missed of defrauding the Revenue. Various people were required to collect the assessments of tax from their neighbourhoods; if the collector was due for transplantation, he remembered to collect the tax, but he forgot to remit it to Dublin! This form of defalcation was most embarrassing; to pursue the wrongdoer would confer upon him the avoidance of transplantation until his case was determined. The same considerations applied to the retention of witnesses; and little support could be expected from the new proprietors who were only interested in clearing the

surplus Irish off their lands. The Dublin Council warned the
local Revenue officers in March 1654 about this, but much of the
taxes and duties must have been lost by then.

Meanwhile reports were grim from the transplanted Irish who
had already reached Connaught, which was one vast waste.
Successive armies had passed like locusts across it, and what
could not be consumed had been destroyed. Such shelter as
remained, such land as was still cultivated, such resources as
remained were all in the hands of the English soldiers. What was
left was held by the ancient Irish proprietors who were not
enamoured of this invasion by their dispossessed countrymen
from the east. Once the Loughrea Commissioners had allocated
land to a transplantee they were not concerned with how he put
himself into possession, and the ancient proprietors gave the new
arrivals a rough reception. Others, such as toll-keepers and
ferrymen, exploited the situation extorting unfair fees for their
services. News of this soon seeped back across the Shannon, and
lost nothing in the telling. All served to build up resistance to
transplantation and to increase the difficulties of the government
in enforcing their policy. But at the same time the new settlers
were complaining of the profusion of Irish on their lands, and
demanding that the policy should be vigorously enforced. The
council was torn between the conflicting demands of the settlers
and the desire to be merciful, which had the added advantage of
being economically sound. Many Irish went to Connaught,
however, convinced they would be driven there later anyway,
and would fare worse then than now. Many played "loath to
depart", and some managed to get further dispensations to
postpone their moves.

Once the harvest was in during the autumn of 1654, the excuses
of the Irish for failing to transplant were ignored, and if they still
did not go, the English officers had little compunction in driving
them out. On 21 December the Dublin Council reported to
London that "transplantation is now far advanced ... and all
are to be gone by 1 March next". On 27 February 1655 they
published a fresh declaration requiring heads of families to be in
Connaught by 1 March, and to obtain their grant of land there:
they might leave behind their families and servants, but if they
had no allotment of land on which to prepare accommodation,

the latter would be "declared out of protection". Licences for the families to remain would not extend beyond 20 May.

The year 1655 saw a general hardening of the attitude of the English officers: they felt that they had shown considerable restraint in mitigating the full rigour of the law, but that the Irish had not taken advantage of this leniency. Henceforth they would execute the orders of Dublin Castle without question. It was reported from Athy on 4 March 1655 that the officers were "resolved to fill the gaols ... by which this bloody people will know that they are not degenerated from English principles". The leading men might expect to be hanged, and the rest transportation to the West Indies. The government next ordered the crops of those who had failed to transplant to be seized and sold for the benefit of those who had done so. This had insufficient effect, and the general arrest of all untransplanted Irish was ordered. The gaols were crammed, and it became essential to empty them. A few were hanged, many were sent to the West Indies, but the bulk were marched off under escort to Connaught. Before the end of March two men were sentenced to death in Kilkenny for refusing to transplant, and on 3 April Edward Hetherington was hanged in Dublin for this offence, and on his body a placard was stuck reading "For not transplanting".

There now appeared on the scene a book called "The Great Case of Transplantation in Ireland Discussed ... by a Well-wisher to the good of the Commonwealth of England". It was widely known to be the work of Vincent Gookin, an English colonist, one of the six members of Cromwell's Little Parliament of 1653 for Ireland and friendly with both Oliver and Henry Cromwell. He pointed out that the miseries of the Irish could only have deleterious consequences for the English. The success of the resettlement depended largely on the attractions the place would have for the rank and file of the English Army: unless these men stayed upon the scene of their conquests, unless they continued to live in close proximity to each other, then the old Irish proprietors one way or another would return to re-establish their moral ascendancy over the peasantry just as they had after previous plantations. But if the peasantry were exempted from transplantation the English could give them employment, for the great benefit of both. The private soldiers of Cromwell's army who had neither livestock nor the money to buy it, and generally had little agricultural training, would have to depend on the Irish to help them to maintain themselves, improve their estates and leave thriving lands to their posterity. The Irish knew the land, the climate and the techniques necessary to extract the best out of the soil, and to expel them would mean that these lessons would have to be learnt afresh. Irish women knew how to handle hemp and flax, how to make woollen cloth, how best to assist in the running of the farms. The Revenue was already being affected by the transplantation for the taxes were paid from the sale of crops raised by the Irish. Gookin went on to point out that for many of the Irish the exactions of the tax were so great that they were faced with either starvation or taking to banditry. The Irish leadership had already been disposed of, and "forty thousand of the most active spirited men, most acquainted with the dangers and discipline of War" had gone abroad; the priests had been banished. What remained was scarcely a sixth of the original population, and these were "poor labourers, simple creatures, whose sole design was to live and maintain their families, the manner of which was so low that their design was rather to be pitied, than by anybody feared or hindered". He objected to transplantation to Connaught because there the Irish would remain under the influence of their chiefs. He enumerated the difficulties of enforcement, including the violent resistance of the Irish and then asked, "When will this wild War be finished; Ireland planted; inhabitants disburthened; soldiers settled? The unsettling of a nation is easy work; the settling is not. The opportunity for it will not last always; it is now. The soldiers, exhausted with indefatigable labours, hope now for rest. It had been better if Ireland had been thrown into the sea before the first engagement of it, if it is never to be settled."

The book sparked off a crisis. The bulk of the English officers petitioned the Lord Protector, for such was Cromwell's new title, that since parliament had provided for their arrears of pay in Irish land and had undertaken to eject the Irish, the suggestions of Gookin were in effect impertinent; they objected that without transplantation their lands "cannot long be safely enjoyed". Such obstruction would plainly injure the army and unsettle the work of the new plantation. Some officers in Leinster asked for the original orders for the Irish to transplant to be strictly enforced so that honest English might be encouraged to settle among them; they pointed out that the Tories could only be overcome when their sources of food and information were removed, that the Irish were quite capable of revenging an injury of twenty or thirty years standing, and that the settlement of the country would be accelerated by destroying the Irish hopes of recovering their lost lands.

Between these two extreme views of the triumphant English the government blew both hot and cold. The economic necessity of allowing many of the Irish to remain justified the lax enforcement of the new laws; the Puritanical zeal for the suppression of all disorder provoked the periodic round-ups of Irish and the desultory movement of the nation westwards. Gradually but inexorably the Irish were uprooted and packed off to Connaught; by the end of the Cromwellian period the vast bulk had been ejected from the other three provinces, but they were not replaced by a corresponding immigration from England.

The temporary land distribution in Connaught was made permanent by the Athlone Commissioners, officially known as the Court of Claims and Qualifications of the Irish, which began work on 28 December 1654. It was their duty to determine the degree of guilt of every Irish proprietor and to determine the value of the lands he had abandoned east of the Shannon. To ensure that the individual was telling the truth the Commissioners were provided with a mass of government records. The Civil Survey of 1641 set forth the names and estates of all freeholders of that year, the Depositions of 1642 set down the complaints of the dispossessed Protestants after their arrival in Dublin during the first winter of the Rebellion, and these had been cross-referenced and indexed; the records of the Kilkenny Confederacy were available as well as various state papers from Dublin Castle. To Athlone the old proprietor had now to go to obtain his final land settlement. If he was a Protestant and could prove constant good affection to the Parliament of England, he would get a decree restoring him to his estate; but otherwise he would only obtain a certificate for the appropriate proportion of land from which he had been ejected. With this certificate he had to return to the Loughrea Commissioners for a final settlement.

In spite of the vast tracts of Connaught which had been excluded from transplantation, various people obtained grants of land in what was reserved for the Irish. Henry Cromwell was granted Portumna Castle and 6,000 acres as a country residence. Sir Charles Coote also managed to obtain a country estate. Other members of the Athlone and Loughrea Commissioners were not slow to "protect" their own interests; and this provoked the surveyors to behave in a similar fashion. Some of the surveyors went further and required direct or indirect bribes to do their work. Some of the unutterably disheartened Irish could stand the pace no longer; they went mad, or committed suicide, or sold up their pittances for the song offered by the rascally surveyors.

At Michaelmas 1653 the Irish Council had received orders from London to ascertain the extent and value of the lands declared forfeit, and as a result they sent commissioners into every county outside Connaught to investigate those holdings in the hands of the government including Crown and Church land. They summoned juries, and examined on oath all who could give evidence on these matters; agents and bailiffs were required to produce rent books and so on, and to show where boundaries ran. In some places the depopulation was so complete that they were unable to complete their task, and sometimes they had to send to Connaught for the return of some transplantees; this was particularly so in the barony of Eliogarty in County Tipperary. It was as well that they started as early as they did for transplanting was accelerating as they did their work. It was on the basis of this work that tithes and rent charges were determined, that subsequent grants of land were facilitated, and that future tax assessments were made. When it was completed the work was known as the Civil Survey.

On 20 July 1653 the adventurers had their lands allocated by a lottery held at the Grocer's Hall in London. Lots were first drawn to decide the province in which the adventurer should have his satisfaction; then lots were drawn to decide the county. As it was thought desirable for soldiers to be set down alongside the adventurers, each barony was separately assessed and drawn for alternatively by the adventurers and by one of Cromwell's officers on behalf of the soldiers. On the basis of the Civil Survey and the

Grocer's Hall lottery a general council of officers in Ireland then proceeded to draw lots to decide in which province each regiment should settle, then the county and finally the barony. The officers then arranged for Dr William Petty, Physician to the Forces and also a skilled mathematician, to make accurate maps of the forfeited land in the eastern provinces; good maps existed for the bulk of Connaught from Strafford's investigations there fifteen years before. The contract with Dr Petty was signed in the Council Chamber of Dublin Castle on 11 December 1654, after a solemn seeking of God by Colonel Thomlinson. Dr Petty was an agnostic, and privately laughed at the prayers, likening the different Puritan sects to "worms and maggots in the guts of a Commonwealth".

The field work of the survey was performed by the more intelligent and literate soldiers of the army and by the direction of Dr Petty. These men were specially selected as strong and capable of withstanding the hardships inseparable from rock climbing and bog wading. They were also to be competent to "ruffle with" such obnoxious characters as might wish to interfere with their work. Dr Petty undertook to mark out upon his maps every officer's and soldier's lot, but the redistribution of the land was not effected until after the maps were made, and these details were provided by subsequent returns to the Central Chancery. A fire in Dublin in 1711 destroyed these priceless records. If they had been marked on this, the Down Survey, there would have been seen regiment by regiment, company by company, platoon by platoon, the English Army encamped upon almost the very lands they had individually conquered. They were set down without intervals, and without picking or choosing, just as the lot fell.

The lands in the different baronies were listed by the Surveyor-General in a fixed sequence known as a file or a string of con-tiguity. The commissioners for setting out the lands, usually senior army officers trusted by the rank and file, then went to an appointed town for each barony on a specified day, to meet the regiment to be disbanded and allotted its land. In the presence of all ranks the commissioners drew the lots to dispose of the separate landholdings. They drew out only one lot at a time, which was opened and read aloud for all to hear; they then filed the award before drawing the next lot. They thus proceeded, lot by lot, until all the acreage in the barony at the disposal of the Commonwealth had been reallocated. As soon as the lot was drawn all those into whose shares the barony fell had to surrender their debentures or land certificates and they received in exchange a certificate for the actual land they had been granted.

For the distribution of 75,735 acres in County Cork, valued at £60,611 8s 6d, Lord Broghill, Colonel Phayr and two others were appointed as commissioners on 10 January 1654. The baronies were Fermoy, Duhallo, Condon and Orrery; they were required to give seven days' notice of the place and time of drawing lots in Cork, Mallow, Youghal and Bandon. If the number of acres drawn in the lots for any barony exceeded the acreage available, they were to make up the deficiency in the next barony. The officers and men were to take up their allocation immediately; when they had subdivided it among themselves, they were to report the details to the local Revenue officer. On getting possession of their lands their pay would stop.

Although the Commonwealth gave the army its land at one standard rate for each province, the army felt that the distribution amongst themselves should follow a more accurate valuation. A General Council of Officers agreed a revised valuation of the land on 21 November 1653. They assessed the land in Counties Wicklow and Longford at twelve shillings an acre, but that in County Dublin at thirty shillings; nine shillings was felt to be adequate for County Kerry, but twenty-two shillings was the price put on that in County Limerick; eight shillings was the minimum in Ulster, but Antrim and Down were surcharged an extra two shillings and five pence. After this the officers of the different regiments in each provincial lot valued the individual baronies before lotting for these: the records of these valuations have been lost but in the barony of Clanwilliam twenty-two shillings was the assessment, while in neighbouring Kerry five shillings was the revised figure. Finally the lands were revalued yet again as between the different companies or troops.

After the end of the fighting and before the details of the new plantation had been promulgated, the troops continued at their duty stations, but their arrears of pay were allowed to mount in the certain expectation that this could be discharged in land in

due course. This was far from satisfactory for the junior officers
and other ranks, who were hard put to feed themselves, and their
distress steadily increased. Although it was forbidden by the
Ordnance of August 1652, they began to sell their land debentures. As the men were only interested in selling and many officers
were only interested in buying, this prohibition was generally
ignored. The government's record was hardly good, for they
were prepared to advance money on the security of these debentures to the families of those who had been killed on active service.
By the end of 1653 the system had broken down, and a regular
traffic, with brokers and a market rate, had been established for
debentures.

On 1 September 1655 the first and largest of the disbandings
and land settlements took place. The different units chosen for
disbanding were ordered to march with their officers to the region
where their new lands were to be allotted, to disband and to
settle. Charles Fleetwood was well aware that there was some un-
happiness among the troops about this, and he wrote to all
commanding officers concerned on 20 August. "The sooner you
march your men the better; thereby you will be enabled to make
provision for the winter," he said. He concluded in the stately
words of the seventeeth century, "And great is your mercy, that
after all your hardships and difficulties you may sit down, and, if
the Lord give his blessing, may reape some fruits of your past
services." Even so, and in spite of the further inducements of a
new suit of clothes, a month's half-pay and possibly allowing
a few Irish to stay behind to help in the resettlement, there was
still trouble in getting the men to accept their lot. The rank and
file found themselves with a tract of some fifty acres, but neither
implements, nor stock, nor money. The Irish had gone, and he
was alone. Under these conditions he was often glad to accept
a trifling sum and his fare home to England in return for the
barren acres which faced him.

Numerous difficulties arose over the allocation of lands to the
adventurers in London. Some baronies had less land for resettlement than was believed to exist in Grocer's Hall; others
had more. The result was confusion. Consequently Dr Petty was
called upon to overhaul these proceedings; he made fresh files of
contiguity and had these arranged so that in due course every

man received full payment for his debenture. The adventurers themselves began to arrive in Ireland in 1656 and continued to come until the Restoration four years later. On arrival they often found their land was still occupied by the Irish; the soldiers on the adjacent land regarded them as unwelcome competitors; and the agents of the government were not interested in their woes. The soldiers, in particular, had no desire to eject the Irish since they provided various services and helped to pay the tax assessments. The Irish, naturally, were not slow to exploit this distrust of the soldiers for the interloping civilians!

The government had reserved all forfeited property in the towns for themselves; this was to pay the general public debt, and to provide an additional annual income from the rents. Between 1652 and 1656 many orders were given to clear all transportable Irish out of the towns, but these orders were generally evaded. All Irish and Catholics were ordered out of Kilkenny before 1 May 1654, excepting up to forty artificers and labourers; every artificer and labourer thereupon claimed to be one of the forty! The local English finding their services cut off gave the government no assistance in enforcing these orders. Sometimes the local commander was authorized to dispense with transplantation orders for a specified period; the Governor of Clonmel issued passes for some artisans to remain until 25 March 1655; the Governor of Dublin was permitted to issue passes for up to twenty days. Even after these licences expired the Irish continued to find excuses to remain; and when they were thrown out of the towns they still remained in the neighbourhood, often sheltered by their English masters who urgently needed their services. But if in a town there was a multi-religious population of artisans, the Protestant faction took full advantage of the political situation to advance their own interests; on 10 October 1656 the Protestant shoemakers of Dublin had their Catholic rivals banished; on 3 April 1657 the coopers objected to Catholic competition, and they were removed as well.

The government continued to make great sweeps to clear out those Irish who should have gone to Connaught but had not done so. In 1656 all Irishmen and Catholics were ordered out of every walled town before 26 May and to stay at least two miles away; in places this was effective. Large numbers of English traders were arriving with the adventurers, and sometimes they found difficulty in obtaining accommodation because the Irish had not been ejected. On 15 May 1655 it was ordered that the forfeited houses in Kilkenny should be let to "English and Protestants and none others". At the same time English merchants were forbidden to trade through "Irish agents or servants"; ejected Irish were given twenty days to leave for Connaught. But there were difficulties; the English merchant had come to Ireland to enjoy a good life, and the Irishman could do all the hard work; why should the Englishman throw out the Irish worker?

It was in house property in the towns that the government paid off the bulk of their debts. Captain John Arthur was owed £3,697 10s and he agreed to accept forfeited houses in Wexford. Just as in the case of the soldiers so was Captain Arthur required to make his choice of where to begin, and then take the houses in order on each side of the street until his due proportion was reached. But it was now that the troubles of the government began in earnest; the new landlords wanted tenants for their new estates who could pay an annual rent, but the only available tenants were transplantable Irish. What were they to do? They consulted their pockets, and let the property to Irishmen.

Although the government had taken strong measures from the very beginning of the reconquest, pushing forward their policies of transplantation and encouraging the disgruntled to go abroad, there were still young Irishmen for whom the ancient hatred of the English coupled with the spectacle of defeat, despair and degradation was a sufficient reason to continue resistance, although the consequences of being caught were distinctly unpleasant. They saw their countrymen return home only to leave again forever; they saw with shame the presence of the triumphant English soldiery; they saw the whole country given over to full English exploitation. Under the leadership of dispossessed gentry and some Irish officers who had escaped, they took to the bogs and hills to live the life of a bandit, the Irish Tory. Their principal object of attack was livestock, so that they could live in the wilds, but occasionally they took to killing individual Englishmen. Periodically, too, the English went in search of Tories; if they were caught, short was their shrift.

To stop the Tories the government was prepared to be very harsh indeed. In March 1655 John Symonds and his two sons who had just arrived to settle at Kilnemarne, were repairing some buildings on their farm when they were attacked by some Irish; one son was murdered and the other badly wounded. The dead son left a widow in very straitened circumstances and charitable subscriptions were invited for her relief. The government specially drafted a party of soldiers to the area with strict orders to uproot all the Irish and pack them off to Connaught under escort. But in spite of this exemplary punishment two Protestants were murdered on 22 October at Lackagh a few miles away. A more severe punishment was meted out this time: four Irish were hanged for not preventing the murder; the rest, including two priests and an eighty year old woman, were transported to the West Indies.

The more usual depredations of the Tories concerned property, and to stop this the government levied a compensatory contribution on all the Irish of the neighbourhood whenever livestock were taken. The Irish were often too poor to pay, and then the contribution would be made up from neighbouring areas. The result was to increase the numbers of Tories, because the grinding taxation coupled with the depredations of the Tories and the consequent compensation payments drove many Irish to the view that it would be better to take their chance with the outlaws rather than face certain ruin from both sides if they stayed at home. A price was put on the heads of some Tories, the greater outlaws being priced at thirty pounds and the small fry at a mere twenty shillings. Sometimes to quieten a district a local gentleman would be spared from transplanting in return for Tory-hunting. Major Charles Cavanagh was allowed to stay in County Carlow with thirteen assistants, and they kept that area quiet.

Wilder and more desperate men "ran out" to become Tories. A natural leader of them was Gerald Kinsellagh who had owned 1,420 acres in County Carlow; this had been declared forfeit and he had been ordered to Connaught. Instead he took to the wilds where he remained at large until 1659 when the government offered him and two others their security and liberty if they would hunt down other Tories who were menacing the district. This was a generally effective way of dealing with the matter: if any other Tory cared to surrender after killing two of his comrades, he would be pardoned.

Twelve years of disorder had permitted the fauna of Ireland to increase in ways inimical to man. Without hunting, wolves and deer had multiplied, and by the end of the war the former were a serious menace. Irishmen were specially employed to hunt them, and these men were exempted from the usual restrictions. By an order dated 29 June 1653, and repeated on 1 July 1656, the various army commanders had to appoint special days for wolf-hunting. Whoever brought in a head to the Revenue officers was rewarded with £6 for a bitch, £5 for a dog, £2 for a cub and 10s for a sucking cub. These predators were so numerous that the bounty payments became a serious charge on the Treasury. Only nine miles from Dublin itself a pack of wolfhounds was kept to rid the land of these vermin.

Deprived of the society of their own kith and kin by years of war followed by defeat and the schemes for clearing the land of the young men, the Irish girls sought husbands from among the fresh arrivals. These young soldiers were equally deprived of lady friends from England by the combination of the disturbed state of the country and the disinclination of the English girls to risk visiting such a wild place. Previous attempts to control Ireland by vast plantations had failed due to the attractions which the Irish maidens had for the colonists. The English commanders, well aware of this danger, took steps to avoid it. They began by ordering the chaplains of the different regiments to preach against the habit of fraternizing with any Irish at all, and to remind the troops that as Christians they must not form any sort of irregular union with any woman whatsoever. Generally in the early days of the Cromwellian campaign the troops were kept on the move too much for any liaisons to develop, but later when sieges and garrison work kept the men in one place the opportunities presented themselves; and the men would not have been human to have missed them.

On 1 May 1651 Henry Ireton issued an order to the army drawing attention to the practice and warning all concerned against marrying Irish girls who were Papists, "or who only for some corrupt or carnal ends pretend to be otherwise." He went on, "Though a real change in the blind deluded people . . . were to be

12

wished and ought to be endeavoured by all good people . . . yet that none be left to their own misguided judgements . . . I think fit to let all know that if any officer or soldier of this army shall marry with any woman of this nation that are Papists, or have lately been such, and whose change of religion is not, or cannot be judged . . . to flow from a real work of God upon their hearts . . . I say that any officer who marries any such shall hereby be held uncapable of command or trust in this army, and for any soldier, if a dragoon he shall be a foot soldier, if a foot soldier a pioneer, without hope of promotion, unless God do by a change wrought upon them with whom they have married take off this reproach."

For irregular unions with Irish girls there was more formal punishment. The Long Parliament had made adultery a strict criminal offence, although there was difficulty with some juries; and the army treated it in the same way. A certain Captain William Williamson was court-martialled in March 1654 for committing fornication with a woman in County Tipperary during his service there. Private soldiers were chastised for this offence. Private Powell of Colonel Hewson's regiment was convicted of sexual irregularity with an Irish girl, and was sentenced to "be whippt on the bare back with a whipcord lash, and have forty stripes while he is led through the four companies of the Irish forces before Whitehall . . . and twenty stripes more after that at Putney"; Private William Sword of Venables' regiment was "whippt at the limbers of a piece of ordnance in Windsor, from the Castle gate to the Churchyard gate, in the High Street, and back again, with a whipcord lash" for the same offence.

But a far more serious breach in Puritan policy came from the officers in temporary possession of the forfeited estates. When they arrived on the estate they often found the previous owner if not in the mansion house at least in the close neighbourhood. Most of the officers were bachelors; many of the old proprietors were surrounded by their families. In these remote places the only society available to the officers were the old gentry. The officer and his predecessor would possibly have fought in the same battle; but now that the fighting was over, they would naturally become friends. Each would find the other more congenial company than the soldiery or the peasantry, and under these circumstances the officer soon fell for the charms of Ireland. The daughter of the old proprietor was not averse to becoming the wife of the new land-lord. This process was so rapid that in 1652 when the first arrangements were being made to pay the troops in land it was suggested that any officer or man who married an Irishwoman should be deprived of his arrears. This was not taken up because the women were ordered to Connaught with the men. But the very people upon whom the government depended to enforce these orders were the closest friends of the girls! "Planted in a wasted country amongst the former owners and their families, with little to do but to make love, and no lips to make love to but Irish, love or marriage must follow between them as necessarily as a geometrical conclusion follows from the premises."

Immediately they obtained possession of the land, the officers took Irish tenants to work the estate since there were no English to do so. As the necessity of tillage increased, so did the necessity of keeping the Irish on the spot. The first tenant was often the old landlord, and the officers connived at their avoidance of trans-plantation. On first hearing about this in Limerick on 1 June 1655 Charles Fleetwood revoked all former dispensations and ordered the strict policy to be applied. He fixed three months as the period for the unconditional execution of his orders. Reaching Dublin two months later he learnt that procrastination was still the case in Munster; furious, he threatened that further procrastination would be treated as grave dereliction of duty. But it was too late. The officers still sheltered the old gentry, and when investigations came too close, they arranged things with their neighbours that matters were concealed. Even if the old proprietor was rounded up and sent to Connaught, the daughter often remained to preserve the Irish tradition, Ireland had woven her irresistible charm around these officers; henceforth their interests were Irish. Protestants themselves, their Irish wives were Catholic at least in thought; in due time their children would embrace the Roman faith.

The Irish cause had been sustained at certain periods by the Presbyterian Scots from Ulster. Fleetwood and some of his senior officers felt that they, too, should be transplanted: they lived in close proximity to their homeland, and could be sustained by pernicious doctrines from Ayrshire and Galloway. In 1653 they sent Colonel Venables and four others to Carrickfergus, before whom these Scots were to take a new oath of allegiance to the state being one without a king. They had little success, and as a result 260 of the leading people were ordered to move to counties Kilkenny, Tipperary and Waterford, where they would be fully compensated for the land they held in Ulster; their ministers might accompany them. But before these orders were carried into effect Cromwell dissolved the Long Parliament and with it the authority behind the move. The Scots of Ulster were reprieved; their most dangerous hour had passed, and they remained in Antrim and Down, as their descendants do to this day.

With the Land Settlement went a Grand Assize. The Puritans were determined that those responsible for the original rising and the atrocities should be prosecuted for their crimes. They were prepared to draw a veil across much, particularly if done by subordinates, but for the leaders the usual severe punishment must be meted out. Of the original conspirators most were beyond the reach of parliamentary justice. Owen Roe O'Neill had died; Emer MacMahon and Sir Henry O'Neill had been hanged after the battle of Scarriffhollis; Lord Maguire and Hugh MacMahon had been hanged at Tyburn; Phil O'Reilly had been allowed to go abroad. But Sir Phelim O'Neill, Archbishop Edmund O'Reilly, Lord Muskerry and Lord Mayo were still in Ireland; the necessary evidence was still available, and so orders were issued for their arrest and trial. Dr John Jones, one of the regicides and now on the Council of Ireland, was instructed to collect the necessary testimony; Chief Justice Lowther assisted by collecting documents and taking depositions; and Dr Henry Jones, the Scoutmaster-General, formerly Bishop of Clogher and later of Meath in the Anglican hierarchy of Ireland, also helped, and this was especially valuable for his knowledge of the country was unrivalled.

In October 1652 a High Court was set up at Kilkenny under the presidency of General Reynolds. It sat in the very room used by the Confederate Catholics as their Council Chamber. The first to be tried was Walter Bagenal, who had assisted in the execution of a William Stone as a spy in May 1642; he was convicted of being an accessory to murder, and shot. Fifteen others were convicted at Kilkenny and executed; six more were dealt with at Clonmel, and a further thirty-two at Cork. This work kept three judges busy until January 1653, when they returned to Dublin.

Sir Phelim O'Neill had not gone abroad after the capture of Charlemont, but had gone to live at Coalisland in County Tyrone with his wife. He was now arrested and taken to Carrickfergus, where Colonel Venables treated him as a brave enemy, and then on to Dublin. Here at the end of February 1653 he was arraigned for high treason and murder: there was no defence to the first charge, but the prosecution wished to prove the delinquency of the second as well and they pressed their charge of the murder of Lord Caulfield. Caulfield had been surprised and captured at Charlemont on the first day of the rebellion there and he had been kept a prisoner there for five months, and then Sir Phelim had ordered his removal to Cloughoughter. The first day's journey took Caulfield and some other prisoners to Kinard; the escort was tired and suspicious; to avoid the necessity of watching their prisoners they decided to kill them, and all were butchered. Sir Phelim's subsequent behaviour was inconsistent with innocence. Many other murders were done in his area, and he took no steps to stop them, nor to punish those responsible. Michael Harrison, a Protestant, had saved his own life by agreeing to act as Sir Phelim's secretary. He swore that he had heard Sir Phelim declare that Mass should be said in every church in Ireland and that not a single Protestant should be left alive in the country. He went on to say that it was at Sir Phelim's orders that he erased the writing from the Royal charter after which the sham commission had been forged. There was ample evidence to sustain Sir Phelim's conviction on both counts, and he was sentenced to the usual traitor's death. His associate, Tirlogh Groom O'Quin, was executed a few days later.

Lord Mayo was arraigned at Dublin in December 1652 for his share in a massacre at Shrule in February 1642. Under the terms of his surrender he was entitled to be tried in Connaught, and when he brought this fact to notice, his trial was removed to Galway. A special commission, consisting of Sir Charles Coote, Colonel Peter Stubbers, who according to tradition was the actual executioner of King Charles I, and nine others, sat to try Mayo. He had undoubtedly witnessed the massacre; he could probably have stopped it; and he could certainly have punished those responsible. His conviction, by seven votes to four, appears to have been more for cowardice than for being an accessory to murder. He was shot.

After the surrender of the Irish forces in County Kerry, Lord Muskerry had gone to Spain, where his reception had been unfriendly, probably due to the internal Irish feuds. He returned to Ireland in February 1653, but he was arrested and brought to trial in the following December charged with complicity in three murders. On two counts he was acquitted, but on the third the prosecution was held to have proved the facts. However Muskerry showed that he had no real responsibility for what was done, and that he had also alleviated a lot of unnecessary suffering. Consequently his judges felt obliged to order his release, and he then left Ireland for ever.

But the most remarkable of these cases was that of Edmund O'Reilly, Vicar-General of Dublin and later Archbishop of Armagh, who was charged with the murder of John Joyce and others at Wicklow in December 1642. They had been burnt in Wicklow Castle and O'Reilly had been present. The evidence against him was very dubious and mainly secondhand. One witness admitted that O'Reilly had excommunicated him for living in adultery, which rendered all his testimony suspect. On the other hand five Protestant clergymen had been saved by O'Reilly's intervention. It appeared that he had supported the rising at first, but later had been revolted by the excesses. He was found guilty and sentenced to death, but the Irish Council pardoned him and he went free. Such favour to a Catholic priest was widely believed to be due to the provision of timely information to Michael Jones just before the battle of Rathmines. It is now known, too, that he had acted as an agent in the secret negotiations between Jones and Owen Roe in 1648. To requite these acts by executing O'Reilly would have been both treacherous and inhumane.

About two hundred people were hanged, shot or beheaded by sentence of the courts for their part in the original uprising or for some subsequent atrocity. The courts admitted much evidence unacceptable in the normal course of events; without some straining of the rules their position would have been impossible; nevertheless such favour as they showed was on the side of mercy, and they handed down to Ireland a doctrine of maintaining the ascendancy of the law over the rough reprisal even though this had been richly deserved.

Cromwell's plans for Ireland were not just punitive; he knew that in addition to providing a new upper and middle class from England he must wean the peasantry from their leaders, material and moral. He would have to make the country prosperous and stable before he could relax his hold; and he would have to direct the energies of the new nation into courses acceptable to England. If Ireland remained dependent, the power in the land would exploit the position for its own narrow and corrupt ends; if she were truly independent, the potential menance to England's sea power would be enormous. But if the two countries became one, their interdependence would represent a real accretion of strength, economic and military, to both.

The supreme authority in England was the Long Parliament, but it was too large to control the Executive. Cromwell and his senior army officers had long been dissatisfied with its dilatory ways, factions, scandals and quarrels. In April 1653 Cromwell could stand no more; with the backing of Major-General Harrison and some troops, he dissolved the remnant of that body in an angry speech, still remembered and still quoted. Publishing his reasons for this he remarked that "it had pleased God . . . to reduce Ireland", but he gave no indication of what he intended. Six weeks later he summoned a nominated assembly of 140 members, of whom six represented Ireland. This, Barebone's Parliament, sat for five months and produced the Instrument of Government, which provided for a parliament of 453 members, of whom thirty would be elected by Ireland.

On 27 June 1654 Cromwell ordered elections to be held in Ireland, specifying the constituencies and nominating the places where they should he held. These took place at the end of August. Colonel Hewson was returned for counties Meath and Louth; Lord Broghill, Colonel Jephson (who wanted Cromwell crowned) and Vincent Gookin represented the towns and county of Cork; and Coote obtained the seat for Galway. This parliament met on 3 September 1654, but Cromwell dissolved it on 22 January 1655. Fresh elections produced no real change in the Irish representation for Cromwell's last parliament. These arrangements were designed to prove that Ireland was no longer a dependency, but part and parcel of the Commonwealth. There was free intercourse between the separate parts; no customs duties were levied on goods passing from one country to another; the excise was uniform; the same heavy taxes were payable in Ireland as were payable in England.

At the end of 1656 the cost to the Commonwealth of the re-conquest of Ireland was assessed. An abstract was prepared covering the period from 6 July 1649, just before Cromwell landed in Dublin, to 30 November 1656. This showed that England had spent £1,566,848 on maintaining the army; Ireland had borne a taxation of £1,942,548, which included £252,474 from Customs and Excise, but did not include forfeitures and sequestrations. From this the infantry had been paid £1,243,309 and the cavalry £1,305,548; other military charges came to £444,071. The civil charges, including the bounties for wolves, and the salaries of public servants, came to £493,240. After taking into account some other small payments the deficit was only £3,196. But before the days of living on credit and banking this was a serious matter. Indeed Cromwell never balanced his books, although careful administration was leading the Commonwealth into solvency.

Henry Cromwell replaced Fleetwood as President of the Irish Council in September 1655; his regiment had been in Ireland since the days of Drogheda, and he himself had returned a few weeks previously. His principal concern in government was to be moderate, and to risk antagonizing as few of the new colony as possible. The wilder spirits were disgruntled at having to behave themselves, but the bulk of the populace were glad that regular proceedings were replacing ruthless military exactions. This produced a satisfying tranquillity in the turbulent scene. It was his policy to produce a new class of whom all "will have too great interests in forfeited lands to give them up to Charles Stuart or any from him". In November 1657 Henry became the Lord Deputy, and all administration was carried out in his name.

On the anniversary of his victories at Dunbar and Worcester, 3 September 1658, Oliver Cromwell died from malaria, originally contracted in Ireland. He was succeeded by his son Richard as quietly as any former King had been succeeded by a Prince of Wales. Richard began by promoting his brother to Lord Lieutenant. Then he issued writs for a new parliament, and again thirty members were returned for Ireland. On 23 March 1659 the House

debated the continued representation of Ireland; some wanted a
separate legislature in Dublin on the ground that Ireland could
not bear the heavy taxes; others opposed this on the grounds that
they represented not Ireland but the English in Ireland whose
language, habits, religion, laws and interests were the same. By
a majority of fifty the representation of Ireland was continued.
But soon Richard Cromwell found that the officers of the army
were resolved to be rid of him, and without any trouble he quit.
Henry's position became more important and more impossible;
however he continued at his post, and under his mild but firm
hand Ireland remained quiet.

After the departure of Richard Cromwell there was no one man
whose authority in the State was unfettered; even Fleetwood, the
commander-in-chief of the army, was dependent on his rival,
General Lambert. The only two officers who might have wrested
control from the London based factions were far away. Henry
Cromwell in Dublin and George Monck in Edinburgh between
them disposed of the best soldiers in the Commonwealth; both
were good generals, competent administrators and discerning
politicians. Both knew that sooner or later the military power
would have to be subordinated to the civil administration. In these
troubles Londoners, with the authority conferred by the citizen-
ship of the capital, and with the tacit approval of the rest of the
nation, called for the reassembly of the Long Parliament, who had
not consented to their dissolution by Cromwell. Old Speaker
Lenthall and about sixty others were hustled back to the chapel of
St Stephen where they gravely considered the state of the nations.
They desired the presence of Henry Cromwell. He hurried back to
London and told them his story on 6 July 1659. He complained
of his lack of clear orders, but averred that the army in Ireland
was loyal, that "the dangerous, numerous and exasperated people,
the Irish natives and Papists" gave no cause for anxiety, but concluded "I cannot promote anything which infers the diminution
of my late father's honour and merit." He then retired into private
life. He might easily have headed a movement to place himself at
the head of affairs, to have sustained the Royal cause, to have
supported Fleetwood, or to have organized a semi-Royalist party
to negotiate conditions with Charles Stuart. He did none of these
things. Instead he set his father's Ironsides an example; they, too,

would go home to become the stalwarts of their society, as respected in peace as they had been feared in war.

After the going of Henry Cromwell the government of Ireland was carried on by five commissioners, and Ludlow was appointed to the command of the army. With £30,000 provided from London he paid off some of the soldiers' arrears, and he smartened up their discipline. Some officers were "guilty of habitual immoralities" and were "debauched in their principles"; others had married Irish Papists. He remedied this, and almost immediately afterwards was called upon to provide troops for the suppression of trouble in England. He sent Sir Hierome Sankey with 1,500 troops to Cheshire; although the men were all English, they were known as the Irish Brigade. In spite of this departure of troops, and the disgruntlement of some of the wilder military spirits in Dublin, Ireland remained quiet, and continued so.

On 1 January 1660 Monck with the army of Scotland at his back crossed the Tweed at Coldstream and began his celebrated march to London, nominally to declare for a free parliament, but actually to arrange for the return of Charles Stuart. New commissioners were appointed for Ireland and these were Lord Broghill, Coote and Major Bury. They summoned a Convention Parliament in Dublin in February. Things now started to move fast. Both countries were fed up with the constant anarchy and tired of changes in supreme authority and on 8 May 1660 Charles Stuart was proclaimed King in London; six days later this was repeated in Dublin. The leaders of the moderate party were rewarded for their success: Monck was created Lord Lieutenant, with Sir Maurice Eustace the new Lord Chancellor, Coote and Broghill as Lords Justice; the soldiers were ennobled, the former as the Earl of Mountrath and the latter as the Earl of Orrery.

The Cromwellian era was over: the King had been restored. Under his new dispensation Ireland, old and new, expected more than it was possible to provide. All had claims to the new King's favour: the new occupiers of the land could say they had settled it, and more recently had sustained Monck; the Ormonde faction could say they had supported the King through thick and thin and had been Protestant upholders of the Royal cause; the Catholics could point to their sustenance of resistance to

Cromwellian conquest and their consequent material disaster. How well King Charles II requited these favours compares most unfavourably with the single-minded determination of his unique predecessor.

The great work describing the Cromwellian land settlement is that of:
  C. Prendergast: *The Cromwellian Settlement of Ireland* (1862).
Prendergast was Irish, Catholic and Nationalist; nevertheless he gives a fair picture of the situation as it must have existed during the period of the Commonwealth.
The physical side of the survey is described in the *Life of Sir William Petty*.
Cromwell's work in writing a Constitution for the whole Commonwealth is described in:
  S. R. Gardiner: *History of the Commonwealth and Protectorate*.
  C. H. Firth: *History of the Later Protectorate*.
This is documented in Gardiner's *Constitutional Documents* and:
  J. Scobell: *Acts and Ordinances of the Protectorate*.

CHAPTER 8
Epilogue

CHARLES STUART was restored to the thrones of his ancestors in May 1660. He landed at Dover with his brother James, Duke of York, to enjoy a triumphal reception greater than that conferred upon Oliver Cromwell on his return from Ireland. His route was obstructed by cheering multitudes, who were only too anxious to exhibit that self-same loyalty that had sustained Cromwell in his prime; the road to London became a scene of joy unknown since the days of Queen Elizabeth. At Blackheath drawn up to receive their new monarch were the veterans of the army of Scotland; these were some of the very men who had hunted the King after the battle of Worcester, and there were some too, no doubt, who had helped to bring his father to his ignominious end on the scaffold. Neither drew much comfort from the sight of the other; for the soldier, Charles represented retribution for his officers whom he respected; for Charles, the soldiers were the ever present reminder that one false move, one hasty angry word, one piece of unwarrantable arrogance, and he would be lucky if he escaped to the safety of a penurious exile. "One hour of their beloved Oliver . . ." was no idle threat, and well did the new King know it. Yet before his gaze was that instrument of policy for which Cardinal Mazarin had begged, which had driven a Pope a thousand miles away to alter his instructions, which had compelled the tyrants of North Africa to disgorge their loot, which had defeated the finest infantry of Spain behind fortifications described by the ablest soldiers of Europe as impregnable, and which had imposed upon their own countrymen a morality as rigid as that of any

monastic order and as strictly enforced as their own military
discipline. The future of this magnificent army, one of the finest
the world has known, was one of the first problems which faced
the King.

To commence his reign the King permitted his fawning minions
to deal the commanders of the Commonwealth Army, other than
Monck and his supporters, the very sharpest blow possible; in
this the law was able and willing to assist. All who had signed the
death-warrant of King Charles I were undoubtedly guilty of
treason, but about one-third were dead and another third had
fled; the remainder were tried for their lives. The consequences
were neither in accordance with the wishes of the government nor
in their long term interests. The first to suffer was Major-General
Thomas Harrison; his courage was never in doubt, and to the last
it was sustained by a ferocious fanaticism worthy of Oliver himself. The Tyburn crowd who had come to mock and jeer were
silenced by the proud and indeed truculent bearing of the condemned man; he had faced death and triumphed in the past;
that he would be vanquished now was not even a matter for
regret. Sir Hardress Waller, convicted at the same time, had his
sentence commuted to life imprisonment in Jersey. Colonel Goffe
escaped to Massachusetts, where it is said that he organized the
defence of part of the colony against attacks by marauding
Indians. Hugh Peters, the chaplain, was hanged; but General
Lambert's life was spared, and he died a prisoner in Plymouth in
1684. George Monck, however, was rewarded with a dukedom,
and his brother with a bishopric.

Oliver Cromwell, Henry Ireton and John Bradshaw were dead,
and had been buried amongst the kings in Westminster Abbey.
This was too much: they were exhumed and on 30 January 1661,
the twelfth anniversary of the execution of King Charles I, their
bodies were dragged on sledges to Tyburn. There they were hanged
"at the several angles of that triple tree, where they hung till the
sun was set; after which they were taken down, their heads cut off,
and their loathsome trunks thrown into a deep pit under the
gallows". The common hangman put their heads on poles which
he then set on the highest pinnacles of Westminster Hall. In spite
of all rumours and legends the dust of Oliver Cromwell, Lord
Protector of the three nations, lies somewhere beneath the soil

in Connaught Square, a fitting epitaph to the repopulator of that disordered province. His head remained on Westminster Hall until a gale one night over a hundred years later blew it down; it was picked up by a soldier who sold it for the price of a drink; it fell into the hands of the Wilkinson family who kept it for a further hundred years as an heirloom, before it was privately immured in the wall of the chapel of Sidney Sussex College, Cambridge, where he had once been an undergraduate. The public dishonour done to Oliver's body may have given satisfaction to the Irish Catholics: it was all they received. But thinking men were disgusted by this ghoulish trend of public behaviour, which, however gratifying to the resurgent vanquished, made neither sense at home nor honour abroad. Cromwell had established the fame of Britain on a dizzy pinnacle; Charles would bring about the descent into the abyss.

The new men at the head of affairs, sustained by the vast bulk of the nation, were agreed that they would not find the money to maintain in arms one man more than was vitally necessary. Thus with the exception of one guard regiment, now the Coldstream Guards, the foot and horse of the Commonwealth were disbanded. The Cromwellian veterans in England were as assuredly dispersed across the land as their counterparts in Ireland, with the difference that in England they were not the new elite, only the old masters. These men took with them into retirement a reputation, which no denigrator can ever sully, for sobriety, probity, character and dignity which served their new monarch far better than he deserved. They set up a standard for incorruptibility which we still endeavour to emulate; and above all they carried home that concept of duty which derives its satisfaction from seeing a task properly performed. With them into the oblivion of retirement went the less obnoxious senior officers. Colonel Venables virtually disappeared before he died in 1687; Charles Fleetwood and John Desborough finally settled down to enjoy an old age which stretched into the days of King William III and Queen Mary II. But Ludlow's adventures were stormy; although he was a regicide, his life had been spared, but he felt it would be wise to leave the country and in this he was wise. The government changed its mind and ordered his arrest; but he had reached the safety of France. He went on to Switzerland where he wrote his

memoirs and where Royalists tried to kill him. When James II
was deposed he returned to London. His presence became known
and the new government ordered his arrest, but he slipped out of
their clutches once more and returned to Switzerland. Before he
died in 1693, he had seen the Britain of modern democracy, the
State which would rather not acknowledge any debt to her re-
publican past or her regicidal army officers.

The financial arrangements and the redistribution of land were
thorny problems; and they were solved differently in Ireland. In
overthrowing everything Cromwellian, the good and bad went
together; thus the Irish Parliament was called back into being and
the legislative union postponed for nearly another century and a
half. Under the terms of the Declaration of Breda, Charles II had
promised "a free Parliament, by which . . . we will be advised";
he would ask this body to indulge "tender consciences . . . in
matters of religion"; parliament would draw an act of oblivion
over the past; and it would sort out the land question to "provide
for the just satisfaction of all men". This was the policy document
on which the English and Irish Parliaments were to work.

The first concern of the Irish Parliament was to cut down the
financial burden of the army. To do this they imposed a poll-tax;
every man, according to his social status was required to pay a
sum between a shilling and eight pounds. The revenue from this
with a further £50,000 borrowed from England paid off upwards
of 1,750 officers and men. Nearly two years' arrears remained for
those who stayed on under arms, but as these amounted to less
than 2,000, the raising of the necessary revenue to pay them off in
due time presented no great problem. But the most important
consequence was that the soldier could no longer impose his
solution on the problems of the nation.

The policy for the new Irish Land Settlement was presented to
the Irish Parliament in November 1660; it was known as "The
Declaration". This acknowledged that the King was bound by
the original statute of March 1642, and it confirmed the adventurers and the soldiers generally in the possession of their lands.
Church lands were excepted, and alternative grants were made
for the occupiers; the same applied to Protestants who had been
dispossessed. The Irish landlords who had been deprived of their
land merely for being Catholics were allowed to have their old

land back if they had gone to Connaught and surrendered their grants there, but only if they applied for this before May 1661. If however they had gone abroad, they could have their land back as soon as the present occupier had been compensated elsewhere; Lords Clanricarde, Taafe, Mountgarret and some others were specially named for restoration of their estates. Ormonde, Inchiquin and some other Royalist Protestants with the Cromwellians who had supported the Restoration, such as Mountrath and Orrery, were confirmed in all their possessions. The utter impossibility of doing right by every man was generally accepted, and insufficient was done for the Irish Catholics for them to acknowledge the fairness of the solution; but those in Connaught were permitted to re-cross the Shannon eastwards to mix with the newcomers on their ancestral lands. Charles II expressed the hope that mutual forbearance would bring about a good understanding between the two antagonistic parties whose common ground was mutual hatred; he might have saved his breath.

A commission of thirty-six, all Protestants, was appointed to execute this policy. After a few Catholics obtained orders for their restoration, the judges advised that the policy should be enshrined in an Act of Parliament. Before this could be passed a general election was held, and this returned a majority of the new freeholders, the Cromwellian officers. Their apparent obsequity to the King concealed their determination to protect their own interests; they insisted on supervising the policy of The Declaration. Little was done except to disburden the adventurers of the surplus land they had obtained under the Doubling Ordinance and to redistribute this, primarily to the King's brother, the Duke of York, who with the estates of the regicides was thus seized of 77,000 acres. He requited this acquisition of the bounty of Ireland by becoming one of her most ruthless absentee landlords.

Lord Mountrath died in December 1661, and soon after this it was announced that Ormonde, now a Duke, would be reappointed Lord Lieutenant. He returned to Ireland in July 1662; his first task was to give the Royal Assent to the Resettlement Act. The Court of Claims which was set up under the terms of this enactment gave judgement for two of the three Catholic claimants who appeared on the first day: this was more than enough for the Cromwellians, and there was trouble. This began with general

obstruction, but after two years a plot was hatched by the hot-
headed new settlers. Known as "The Phanatick Plot", it came to
nothing, with the principals dying on the gallows. Even so, this
was one more mark of the lack of confidence of the new landlords,
in the government. Suddenly the Earl of Antrim asked the Court
of Claims for a decree of innocency; he was sustained by Queen
Henrietta Maria for altruistic reasons and by his creditors in the
hope of recovering their money. In spite of his bad record dating
from the days of Strafford, he obtained the decree and with it the
restoration of 100,000 acres. The distrust of the government was
finally overcome by a Bill of Explanation in 1665; under this the
newcomers were to surrender one-third of their land, but the first
claimants to this were to be the dispossessed Protestants, "of
whom His Majesty ever had and still hath the greatest care and
consideration in the settlement of this his kingdom."

Ireland, after twenty-four years of upheaval, had reached the
end of a hard road; the land, now in the hands of new men of
alien extraction, had been resettled, and this was expected to last.
So far as all the conflicting claims could be reconciled, so far as
the more important people had not been dispossessed and out-
raged, some rough justice had been done. But nations are not
settled by rough justice; there must either be full justice or none
at all. King Charles should have either allotted half the land to the
Catholics and half to the Protestants; or he should have given all
to the one. In the former case justice would have been apparent;
in the latter it would not have mattered, for the loser would have
been obliterated. However no obvious policy was followed, and
attempts at compromise only led to further and graver troubles.
In 1665 England left Ireland to slumber: in reality the brew was
just starting to ferment again.

With the separation of the parliaments at the Restoration,
Ireland ceased to be represented at Westminster: she became a
foreign country for some purposes and a conquered dependency
for others. The English Navigation Acts required all cargoes for
the colonies to be carried in English bottoms, and this excluded
the Irish; other forms of protection struck hard at Irish agriculture; this was justified in England by saying that the Irish were
just a lot of rebels, but the English were really striking at their
own kith and kin, driving them into the arms of the hated Papists.

13

The new settlers had gone to Ireland to seek prosperity, but the home country were denying them an opportunity. As a result of these and other pinpricks the Cromwellians began to throw in their lot with the old Irish. Not for the first time and not for the last, the new leadership which had been grafted on to Ireland displayed sentiments which were distinctly Irish. Many had acquired Irish wives, for the Cromwellian inhibitions had gone with the Restoration; more had imbibed Irish thoughts; most were as firmly attached to the soil as their predecessors. The old leadership of the nation had gone; in its place the Irish peasant could look to the triumphant veteran of the Puritan Revolution, and due to the crass idiocy of the English administration, he did not look in vain. Spurned and rejected by his kinsfolk at home, proscribed by the narrow doctrines of the Irish Church, is it surprising that the officer of the Commonwealth should not turn in anger upon the government?

Within thirty years of the Restoration successive stupidities of the English administration had so alienated Ireland that a fresh campaign to reconquer the island had to be fought. It was said that many of the sons of Cromwell's soldiers not only fought on the Irish Catholic side, but many could not even speak English. Once more a punitive land settlement was effected; once more strict anti-Catholic laws were imposed and enforced. This time there was greater consistency and for twenty-five years religious repression and commercial toleration went hand in hand. On the very verge of complete success, the tight grip of Queen Anne's viceroy was relaxed, and the indifference of the Hanoverians permitted the return of the Catholic priesthood by failing to punish their presence. They also permitted the English Parliament to protect England at the price of penalizing Ireland. Once more England imagined that Ireland was slumbering; once more the brew was fermenting; once more there was an explosion; once more there was reconquest and repression. The rising in 1798 was the most dangerous; the leaders were Nonconformist Protestants and Ulster Scots; only Irish incapability saved the English from their own ineptitude.

The Union of 1801, the Great Potato Famine, the Home Rule struggles, the Easter Rebellion, the Settlement of 1922, all these are the affairs of modern Ireland; but Ireland is still one with

her past. Who were the authors and the leaders of these movements? Look at the names, the real names, and look at the surviving photographs of these men; they are nearly all English both
in name and in features; indeed their characters were nearly all
those of Englishmen. The "new" leaders of Ireland were more
Irish than the Irish; they were in very truth the disgruntled
colonists.

By one of those curious quirks of fate, Cromwell has become
one of Ireland's greatest benefactors in all her long and stormy
history. It was Oliver who took to that land the blood which has
served to strengthen character, which has provided leadership,
which has infused moral stiffening. It has been this blood, too,
which spread by three hundred years of Irish life has enabled the
country to achieve a real and practical independence, conditioned
only by inescapable economic and geographic facts.

Cromwell also introduced thoughts on government completely
alien to Milesian concepts; the establishment of the English
Republic in 1649 was the direct precursor of the modern constitution of Eire. What the Irish fought against in the seventeenth
century was to be their hearts' desire in the twentieth. Even the
policy enshrined in the slogan "Sinn Fein" is but a literal trans-
lation into the Erse of the traditional xenophobic attitude, often
hypocritical and always arrogant, of the larger island. In absorb-
ing Anglo-Norman blood, thought processes have been absorbed
as well. Ireland has deserved well of her immigants, and of none
more than that handful of Ironsides who disembarked on the
banks of the Liffey in the summer of 1649.

But above all Cromwell provided the impetus to dissolve the
links with England, with the classic Irish imprecation and oath:
"The Curse of Cromwell on you!"

All human institutions are said to have the seeds of their own
destruction encrusted within their foundations; is there any finer
example?

The trials of the Regicides can be read in the *State Trials*.
The subsequent history of Ireland can be read in many works, but see Leslie's
Irish Tangle, Froude's *English in Ireland*, and D'Alton.

CLOSING NOTE

Of RECENT years footnote disease has been a recognized ailment of biographers and historical writers, for which the accepted antidote has been acceleration to the preface or relegation to the end. I prefer the latter solution because this persuades the serious critic or the student to examine the evidence at his leisure and after he has had the case presented to him. If at the end of the day he still disagrees with my presentation, at least he cannot say that I have ignored the facts. If truth is the closest approximation to exactitude capable of comprehension by the human mind, then the very bulk of facts, interlarded as they so liberally are with comments, glosses, legends, interpolations and guesses, makes the extraction of veracity difficult indeed. In so far as my authorities are inaccurate, exaggerated or bogus, I must necessarily have failed; and in Irish affairs one is usually judged by failure! Nevertheless in presenting this view of the Puritan invasion and eruption into Ireland, I have endeavoured to show up the deficiencies of both sides as well as their quite remarkable consistency and their undoubted courage.

In the first two chapters I have drawn heavily on the works of Miss Wedgwood and the writings of John Borlase, the Lord Justice of 1641. For the third I have depended on Richard Bagwell and Archbishop Rinnuccini. Carlyle's *Letters and Speeches of Oliver Cromwell* have been invaluable, and Firth's monograph on Cromwell's army was essential for the chapter on the Preparation of the Expedition. There are innumerable descriptions of the Storm of Drogheda, probably the best is that in the consecutive issues of the *Nineteenth Century* in 1911 and 1912. The earlier stages of the campaign in the south are fully documented by Cromwell himself and in Ludlow's Memoirs; Bagwell has unravelled the confusion of the sporadic affrays in the concluding stages. Although Prendergast was a Catholic, an Irishman and not unprejudiced, his description of the Land Settlement is masterly, and will remain the classic work of this episode. For the Epilogue I have relied on general works on Ireland, amongst which Shane Leslie's *Irish Tangle* and the writings of Dr Dalton, Froude, Gardiner and Lecky must be specially mentioned.

Index of Persons

Index of Places

[The Provinces of Ireland, the Pale, Dublin, London and the rivers Liffey and Shannon occur so frequently throughout the text that they are excluded from the list.]

Carlingford, L. & T., 12, 115
Carlow, Co. & T., 15, 78, 134, 142, 143, 154, 160, 162, 176
Carrick Island, 153
Carrick-on-Suir, 128, 132, 138
Carrickfergus, 26, 54, 58, 74, 76, 125, 128, 179, 181
Carrigadroghid, 137
Carrigaholt, 151
Cashel, 60, 80, 133
Castleconnel, 148, 149
Castlehaven, 127
Castleishin, 151
Castlelyons, 151
Castlemaine Harbour, 154
Castletownroche, 132
Cavan, Co. & T., 74, 77, 81, 126, 138, 140, 147
Charlemont, 54, 56, 65, 77, 125, 139, 141, 143, 181
Cheshire, 186
Chester, 73
Clanwilliam, Barony of, 172
Clare Castle, 152
Clare, Co., 66, 141, 151, 152, 162
Clear, C., 11
Clogher, 51
Clones, 69, 84
Clonmacnoise, 129, 144, 146
Clonmel, 136, 138, 141, 174, 180
Cloughoughter, 126, 154, 181
Coalisland, 181
Coldstream, 186
Coleraine, 54, 74, 76, 125, 139
Collinstown, 105
Condon, 172
Cork, City & Co., 11, 15, 36, 56, 59, 60, 66, 123, 124, 127, 129, 137, 154, 161, 162, 172, 180, 183
Crofty, Hill of, 60
Cullaville, 84

Derg, L., 148
Derry, City & Co., 52, 54, 74, 76, 83, 85, 103, 105, 115, 125, 139, 140, 141, 145

Devizes, 95
Doagh, 140
Dodder, R., 87
Donegal, Co. & T., 12, 65, 69, 79, 84, 87, 140, 153
Donore, 147
Dove, R., 108, 109
Dover, 188
Down, Co., 58, 125, 162, 172
Drishane, 151
Drogheda, 54, 59, 69, 79, 84, 87, 97, 105–113, 115, 184
Dromagh, 151
Duhallo, 172
Duleek, 106, 109
Dunbar, 184
Duncannon, 123, 126, 142, 147
Dundalk, 59, 69, 79, 84, 115
Dunfermline, 144, 145
Dungannon, 54, 76
Dungan's Hill, 50, 97
Dungarvan, 127, 129
Dungiven, 140

Edgehill, 67
Edinburgh, 33, 57, 185
Eliogarty, Barony of, 170
Ennis, 145, 151
Enniscorthy, 117, 132, 133
Enniskillen, 52, 55, 56, 84, 138, 140, 141
Ennisnag, 136
Erne, Ls. & R., 55, 140

Ferbane, 146
Ferboe, 149
Fergus, R., 151
Fermanagh, Co., 52, 56, 138
Fermoy, 69, 172
Ferns, 117
Fethard, 133, 135, 138
Finea, 126, 147, 148, 151
Finglas, 84, 85
Folka, R., 85
Foyle, L. & R., 12, 140